The Face of East European Jewry

WEIMAR AND NOW: GERMAN CULTURAL CRITICISM

Edward Dimendberg, Martin Jay, and Anton Kaes, General Editors

The Face
of East European Jewry

Arnold Zweig

With Fifty-Two Drawings by Hermann Struck

Edited, Translated,
and with an Introduction by Noah Isenberg

UNIVERSITY OF CALIFORNIA PRESS

Berkeley   Los Angeles   London

University of California Press
Berkeley and Los Angeles, California

University of California Press, Ltd.
London, England

Library of Congress Cataloging-in-Publication Data

Zweig, Arnold, 1887–1968.
   [Ostjüdische Antlitz. English]
   The face of East European Jewry / by Arnold Zweig ;
with 52 drawings by Hermann Struck ; edited, translated,
and with an introduction by Noah Isenberg.—2nd ed.
     p.   cm. — (Weimar and now ; 35)
    ISBN 0-520-21512-5 (cloth : alk. paper).
    1. Jews—Europe, Eastern—Identity. 2. Jews—
Europe, Eastern—Social life and customs. I. Isenberg,
Noah. II. Struck, Hermann, 1876–1944. III. Title.
IV. Series.

  DS143.Z913   2004
  305.892'4047'09041—dc22   2003019003

Manufactured in the United States of America
13 12 11 10 09 08 07 06 05 04
10 9 8 7 6 5 4 3 2 1

*It does not appear inappropriate to point out
that Hermann Struck, while he was in
partial agreement with the views expressed,
had to allow the author complete freedom and
therefore cannot be held responsible for certain
opinions and emphases. In saying that,
I dedicate this book to my parents.
Arnold Zweig*

CONTENTS

PREFACE TO THE ENGLISH EDITION

> I certainly understand how the average German Jew no longer
> feels a kinship to the Eastern Jews; indeed, he has really lost it
> for the most part, as he has become more philistine, more
> bourgeois. But I, and people like myself, must feel this kinship
> in an unmitigated way.
>
> Franz Rosenzweig

In summer of 1917, during the late stages of battle in the First World
War, a young German writer named Arnold Zweig (1887–1968) was stationed on the Eastern front as a soldier in the special wartime press division at Ober-Ost. There, just outside the Lithuanian city of Kovno
(Kaunas), Zweig was able to fulfill his "extraordinarily intense wish to
experience the Eastern Jews personally."[1] A onetime national patriot and
fully assimilated member of the German-Jewish educated elite, Zweig—
in a change of faith not altogether uncharacteristic among Jews of his
generation—embraced the opportunity to discover a more vital form of
Jewish life distinctly removed from that to which he had been accustomed

1. Arnold Zweig, letter of 15 February 1917 to Martin Buber, cited in Georg
Wenzel, ed., *Arnold Zweig 1887–1968: Werk und Leben in Dokumenten und Bildern*
(East Berlin: Aufbau, 1978), 74. For a more playful account of life at Ober-Ost,
see Sammy Gronemann, *Hawdolah und Zapfenstreich: Erinnerungen an die ostjüdische Etappe, 1916–1918* (Berlin: Jüdischer Verlag, 1924).

in the West. In collaboration with the Zionist artist and printmaker Hermann Struck (1876–1944), likewise stationed at Ober-Ost, Zweig embarked on a project that is known to us today as *Das ostjüdische Antlitz* (*The Face of East European Jewry*).

First excerpted in Martin Buber's acclaimed journal *Der Jude* and then published as a complete book in 1920 (and reissued, slightly revised to include the entire set of drawings by Struck, in a second edition in 1922), *The Face of East European Jewry* appeared at a time when the so-called Jewish Question was fiercely debated. Of paramount concern was the pressing dilemma faced by a considerable segment of the German population: what to make of the rising number of Eastern Jews within Germany's borders and how to view those living both inside and beyond its borders. Zweig's project, then, was to offer an impassioned response— albeit elliptical, lyrical, and given to intense rhetorical flourish—to this dilemma. As he writes in the opening line of his preface to the first edition, "This book about the Eastern Jews is written by somebody who has attempted to observe them." Zweig hoped to demonstrate the strength of the Eastern Jewish community in order to mount a corrective to the prevailing misconceptions of the so-called *Ostjuden*, or Eastern Jews, as degenerate, uncivilized, and essentially devoid of culture.

To read *The Face of East European Jewry* in the twenty-first century is to embark on a journey back in time, a journey that leads us to a very specific juncture within the sweep of modern German-Jewish cultural history. At its core, this juncture signaled a radical turn among otherwise acculturated, bourgeois, German-speaking Jews toward their far more spiritually savvy, traditional-minded counterparts in Eastern Europe. Taking their cue from utopian Zionism and other paths of nationalism, these Western and Middle European Jews, who had up until then invested the bulk of their energy in integration and in the main tenets of modernity, suddenly sought to readjust to the ways of an ostensibly more authentic mode of Jewish existence found in the countless shtetls and small cities of Poland, Lithuania, Russia, and other parts east of Berlin, Prague, and

Vienna.[2] For them, the Eastern Jews offered a striking counterbalance: they spoke their own language; lived in their own community; adhered to the ways of their own tradition and religious practice; and, perhaps most important, they had their own cultural models, heroes, and icons. Even if these rather rosy attributes tended to eclipse the German-Jewish popular imagination—and they were, of course, used in equal measure as terms of veneration and opprobrium—they also help explain the "cult" status accorded to the Eastern Jews, as well as the prodigious output of novels, treatises, articles, and public debate addressing this charged issue. The remarkable little book that Zweig and Struck joined forces to produce in the last year of the Great War is indeed exemplary, if not symptomatic, of this turn among German-speaking Jewry at large.

Arnold Zweig's preoccupations with Eastern Jewry, Zionism, and the dream of Jewish renewal did not begin during his military service on the Eastern front. Born on November 10, 1887, in the Silesian town of Glogau to assimilated parents—his father was a relatively prosperous businessman and his mother part of an established middle-class family—Zweig grew up with the comforts of a modern German-Jewish household.

---

2. For a complete discussion of this historical development, going back to the nineteenth century, see Steven E. Aschheim's seminal study, *Brothers and Strangers: The East European Jew in German and German Jewish Consciousness, 1800–1923* (Madison: University of Wisconsin Press, 1982). See also Sander L. Gilman, "The Rediscovery of the Eastern Jews: German Jews in the East, 1890–1918," in David Bronsen, ed., *Jews and Germans from 1860 to 1933: A Problematic Symbiosis* (Heidelberg: Carl Winter, 1979), 338–365; David N. Myers, "'Distant Relatives Happening into the Same Inn': The Meeting of East and West as Literary Theme and Cultural Ideal," *Jewish Social Studies* 1.2 (Winter 1995): 75–100; and Michael Brenner, *The Renaissance of Jewish Culture in Weimar Germany* (New Haven: Yale University Press, 1996), especially 142–148. On Arnold Zweig's place within this broader cultural context, see my "The Imagined Community: Arnold Zweig and the Shtetl," in *Between Redemption and Doom: The Strains of German-Jewish Modernism* (Lincoln: University of Nebraska Press, 1999), 51–76.

He attended numerous German schools and universities, in Munich, Berlin, Göttingen, and Rostock, finally pursuing (though never receiving) a doctoral degree in philosophy, literature, and philology at the University of Munich. Like many of the more self-conscious German Jews of his generation, Zweig began to discover an interest in Jewish matters around 1911–1912, when he published his short works *Aufzeichnungen über eine Familie Klopfer* (Notes on the Klopfer family, 1911) and *Novellen um Claudia* (1912; English translation, *Claudia*, 1930), both of which deal, to varying degrees, with assimilation and the fate of German-Jewish identity.[3] Zweig's engagement with the Zionist project can be traced to these early years, when he became acquainted with the writings of Buber and started to contribute to such Zionist publications as *Die Freistatt* and to the monumental Bar Kochba anthology of 1913, *Vom Judentum* (On Judaism), a watershed work in the sphere of German-speaking cultural Zionism.[4] Until the outbreak of the war, Zweig's literary career followed a path that steadily drew on Jewish issues and concerns, perhaps most poignantly in his *Ritualmord in Ungarn* (Ritual murder in Hungary, 1914), a tragic play based on a nineteenth-century Jewish blood libel case, for which he received the coveted Kleist Prize in 1915.[5]

---

3. See Arnold Zweig, *Aufzeichnungen über eine Familie Klopfer* (Munich: Albert Langen, 1911); and *Die Novellen um Claudia* (Leipzig: Kurt Wolff, 1912). For a brief overview of Zweig's career as a writer, see my "Arnold Zweig, 1887–1968" in Matthias Konzett, ed., *Encyclopedia of German Literature*, vol. 2 (Chicago and London: Fitzroy Dearborn, 2000), 1032–1034.

4. See Arnold Zweig, "Zum Problem des jüdischen Dichters in Deutschland," *Die Freistatt* 1.5 (August 1913): 375–380; and "Die Demokratie und die Seele des Juden," in Verein jüdischer Hochschüler Bar Kochba, ed., *Vom Judentum: Ein Sammelbuch* (Leipzig: Kurt Wolff, 1913), 210–235. On Zweig's overall engagement with things Jewish, see Hans-Harald Müller, "'Zum Problem des jüdischen Dichters in Deutschland': Arnold Zweigs Auseinandersetzungen mit dem Judentum 1910–1933," in David Midgley et al., eds., *Arnold Zweig—Poetik, Judentum und Politik* (Bern: Peter Lang, 1989), 155–170.

5. See Arnold Zweig, *Ritualmord in Ungarn: Jüdische Tragödie in fünf Aufzügen* (Berlin: Hyperion, 1914).

Zweig's profound and enduring interest in Jewish affairs did not, however, preclude ardent support for the German war effort. In August 1914, he wrote to his friend Helene Weyl (née Joseph), telling her of his extraordinary enthusiasm for what he saw as the "deeply binding power of the cultural community *[Kulturgemeinschaft]*" that had intensified in the war. "Greater Germany is here again," he went on to boast, adding that as a Jew, "I will take passionate interest in Germany's destiny. . . . Indeed, in my inherently Jewish way, I will make Germany's concern my own concern."[6] Curious as it may seem, Zweig had expressed a similar will to make Germany's literary concern his own in his article "Zum Problem des jüdischen Dichters in Deutschland" (On the problem of the Jewish writer in Germany), an amplified defense of German-Jewish authors, of the previous year.[7] His initial wish to stake out a space in the realm of German letters thus carried over into the war years in a new incarnation. Although he immediately volunteered in 1914, he was kept from service, due to bad eyesight, until spring of the following year. Zweig eventually served intermittently in Belgium, Hungary, and Serbia until April 1916, when he was finally stationed in France for over a year. During his first year of service, he remained a loyal *Vaterlandsverteidiger* (defender of the Fatherland), to the point of insisting on being married in uniform in July 1916.

It wasn't long before the devastating blow of the *Judenzählung* (Jewish census, or literally, "Jew count," which sought to monitor Jewish wartime participation), in October of that same year, that Zweig not only began to revise his formerly positive views of the war but also to recognize that it pitted Jews against Jews. As Zweig wrote to Buber, describing the personal insult and betrayal he felt: "The *Judenzählung* was a reflection of unheard sadness for Germany's sin and our agony. . . . If there were no antisemitism in the army, the unbearable call to duty would

6. Arnold Zweig, letter of 27 August 1914 to Helene Weyl, in Wenzel, *Arnold Zweig*, 62–63.

7. See Zweig, "Zum Problem des jüdischen Dichters in Deutschland."

almost be easy. However, to be subjected to such despicable and wretched creatures! I now regard myself personally as a captured civilian and a stateless foreigner."[8] Based on his experiences on the war front, he published the semi-fictional short piece "Judenzählung vor Verdun" (The Jewish census at Verdun) in the Berlin Zionist newspaper *Die Jüdische Rundschau* and, several months later, in the more mainstream publication *Die Schaubühne*. In it, Zweig tells the story of dead German-Jewish soldiers who are summoned from their graves to be counted. They line up, announcing their respective identities as Jews: "Mosaischer Konfession" ("of the Mosaic faith"); "Israelit" ("an Israelite"); "Deutscher jüdischen Glaubens" ("a German of the Jewish faith"); "Jude, ja" ("indeed, a Jew").[9] In a sense, then, the diffuse nature of Jewish life in the West—a concern that lies at the heart of *The Face of East European Jewry*—emerges here in haunting, eerie detail. The Jews in the story represent the extreme gulf separating different kinds of adherents to the faith, Western and Eastern, assimilated and traditional, the same gulf that Zweig himself recognized so acutely. The narrative ends on a plaintive note: "And I awakened from this abrupt, harsh, heart-wrenching horror."[10] To be sure, Zweig's own "awakening," brought about by the *Judenzählung* and the final acknowledgment that Jews were fighting against Jews, was confirmed when, in June 1917, he was transferred to the press division at Ober-Ost.

Upon making the acquaintance of Hermann Struck, Zweig was immediately impressed by the power of Struck's portraiture, which captured for him the unique spirit of the Eastern Jews that he, too, had affectionately observed. Struck, for his part, had long established himself at the forefront of Zionist artists, having completed in 1913 one of the most celebrated portraits of Theodor Herzl, the "countenance of the move-

8. Zweig, letter of 15 February 1917 to Buber, in Wenzel, *Arnold Zweig*, 74.
9. See Arnold Zweig, "Judenzählung vor Verdun," *Die Schaubühne* 13.5 (February 1917): 115–117. The article first appeared in the *Jüdische Rundschau* in November 1916.
10. Zweig, "Judenzählung," 117.

ment."[11] By the time Zweig met him, Struck had already produced, in addition to an extensive cycle of Eastern Jewish profiles, the affecting cover illustration of *Ostjüdische Erzähler* (East European Jewish storytellers, 1916), a collection of classic modern Yiddish fiction and poetry in German translation.[12] In October 1918, Zweig wrote an effusive review of Struck's first volume of etchings, "Strucks 'Ostjuden,'" which in many ways served as a preview of what was to come in the ongoing collaboration between the two. Zweig noted, for example, the artist's "infinite familiarity" with the "law of harmony" and the "politicization of art" that helped enable a better understanding of the Eastern Jews. "The language of the artist is the language of his work," he affirmed in the same review, "the politics of the artist is the sentiment of his form, and is the intensity of the creation and its language."[13] Much the same could be said of Zweig's contribution to *The Face of East European Jewry*, written for the most part as an accompaniment to Struck's illustrations. Both operate from within a specific vernacular shaped around an East-West, Oriental-Occidental axis which serves to convey the same ideological thrust that Zweig highlights in his review.

When Zweig first laid out the plans for his collaboration with Struck, just a few months before the publication of "Strucks 'Ostjuden,'" he eagerly wrote to tell Buber, who, as he likely suspected, would be inclined to share his excitement: "In an already firmly established project, I am

11. See Michael Berkowitz's discussion of Struck's famous portrait of Herzl in *Zionist Culture and West European Jewry before the First World War* (New York: Cambridge University Press, 1993), 131. To be sure, Struck's groundbreaking book, *Die Kunst des Radierens* (The art of etching, 1908; reprinted in 1920) left a lasting mark on the Weimar German and international art scene. For a brief account of Struck's life, see the memoirs of his brother-in-law Henry Pachter, *Weimar Etudes* (New York: Columbia University Press, 1982), 203–207.

12. See Alexander Eliasberg, ed. and trans., *Ostjüdische Erzähler* (Weimar: Gustav Kiepenheuer, 1916).

13. Arnold Zweig, "Strucks 'Ostjuden,'" *Vossische Zeitung*, evening ed., 29 October 1918, 2.

going to write a full account of the Jews of the East, as I have come to know them among the Lithuanian Jews. In a text written in conjunction with some fifty new drawings by Struck, I am going to establish the claim that I now simply write down here: the Jewish human being is indestructible, undistortable, undistractible, is oriented toward purity, sincerity, candor."[14] Most striking about Zweig's letter is his candor concerning the mission—almost a foregone conclusion—of his project, namely, to render a gripping portrayal of the Eastern Jews in highly romanticized, idealized, even utopian terms. In order to achieve this most effectively, Zweig had to rely on a strict dichotomy between the world of Eastern Jewry—marked by such choice catchwords as "purity," "sincerity," and "candor"—and the world of Western Jewry, which for him represented the ultimate site of cultural crisis. If, as he spelled out in his letter to Buber, the chief goal of the book was to establish the claim about the cultural vitality of the Eastern Jews, then his own language, as well as the language of Struck's images, had to be elevated in such a way as to offset the equally lavish claims made by antisemitic ideologues also engaged in the debate.

Along the way toward depicting the Eastern Jews he observed in the Lithuanian towns and cities during his extended "lively cohabitation,"[15] Zweig draws not only on the key terms of an ethnic apologist but also on his own individual understanding of Jewish nationalism and the call for renewal. The text, which he divides into five discrete parts, begins with the figure of the old Eastern Jew and—following excursions into Eastern Jewish institutions such as the place of worship and the home, into labor, politics, and the family—ends with youth, the image of the young Jewish boy as the last beacon of hope. Each section of Zweig's text

14. Arnold Zweig, letter of 13 May 1918 to Martin Buber, in Buber, *Briefwechsel aus sieben Jahrzehnten*, ed. Grete Schaeder, vol. 1, 1897–1918 (Gerlingen: Lambert Schneider, 1972), 534.

15. Moritz Goldstein, "Arnold Zweig," in Gustav Krojanker, ed., *Juden in der deutschen Literatur: Essays über zeitgenössische Schriftsteller* (Berlin: Welt-Verlag, 1922), 249.

is illustrated amply with drawings by Struck that capture the figures and faces of Eastern Jewry, some of which Zweig addresses explicitly, while others are left to stand on their own.

From Zweig's vantage point, the Eastern Jew is to be understood as the exotic other, the living embodiment of an authentic, primal Jewishness derived from myth, lore, and from his very "personal" encounters—a variation, perhaps, of the figure who first entered the German-Jewish imagination in Buber's Hasidic writings from the turn of the twentieth century.[16] Although Zweig declares in his preface to the second edition that he is not a poet, one would hardly know this from some of his more florid, exultant musings:

> Whoever lives simply in the proximity of such matters and such people, whoever protects his soul from giving in to breathless futility, whoever provides lovingly and openly each movement of his hands, each word of his mouth, and whoever gives each connection to his fellow human being and to those brotherly creations a ray of warmth and a friendly heart: he partakes of the redemption of the providence of humankind, which since the beginning of time has been deeply rooted in the providence of the Jew. This great, mature benevolence, the peaceful sincerity of each hour, is commonly visible with profound gentleness among the old Eastern Jews. And sometimes, as one eventually recognizes, they are Hasidim who stand, like ripened pear trees, at the center of the lush, flourishing field of everyday life.

16. On the widespread influence of Buber's Hasidic writings, see Paul R. Mendes-Flohr, "Fin de Siècle Orientalism, the *Ostjuden*, and the Aesthetics of Jewish Self-Affirmation," in his *Divided Passions: Jewish Intellectuals and the Experience of Modernity* (Detroit: Wayne State University Press, 1991), 77–132. With specific regard to Zweig, see Leslie Morris, "Reading the Face of the Other: Arnold Zweig's and Hermann Struck's *Das ostjüdische Antlitz*," in Sara Friedrichsmeyer et al., eds., *The Imperialist Imagination: German Colonialism and Its Legacy* (Ann Arbor: University of Michigan Press, 1998), 189–203; Arthur Tilo Alt, "Zu Arnold Zweigs 'Das ostjüdische Antlitz,'" in Midgley et al., *Arnold Zweig*, 171–186; and Arie Wolf, "Arnold Zweigs Ostjudenbild," *Bulletin des Leo Baeck Instituts* 67 (1984): 15–40.

Large passages of Zweig's text, like this one here, serve as occasions for the author to wax nostalgic, even rhapsodic, about the virtues of the Eastern Jews—virtues that have seemingly been lost in the West in the wake of modernity.

Time and again, Zweig returns to the idea of Eastern Jewish simplicity and the premodern harmony of its lifestyle. The face of the Eastern Jew, Zweig insists, has managed to be preserved over time: it is "sincere and dreamy and of a purity which can be procured only at the cost of sacrificing one's broader activities and the happiness of broader activity." In the process of describing the different aspects of life that most distinguish the Eastern Jew from his German-speaking counterpart, Zweig often doubles back to the fundamental point that "one profoundly feels one's alienation from all that is natural, from all that keeps the Eastern Jew preserved," and as a result, one realizes "how far one is alienated from life itself." Much of Zweig's discussion is aimed at regeneration among the Eastern Jews and the need for Jews in the West to leave behind their bourgeois world in favor of a more meaningful existence. "Renewal: that is what separates us from the others. To the bourgeois Zionist, this renewal remains a physical, possibly a national concern; for us, it is a concern of the human being in its entirety and in its deepest essence, a religious concern. And to the Jew who is faithful to the Torah, it can only serve as a guidepost 'back to the Torah,' to the entire code of law, to life as it once was." On a number of different occasions in his writing— perhaps in an effort to compensate for intense feelings of detachment and alienation—Zweig addresses his Eastern Jewish subjects directly: "[Y]ou are blood from my blood," he avers early on. Somewhat later, and more dramatically, he remarks: "[Y]ou will rise up again transformed and color the red dawn of the times now and then, you will lead and strengthen the dawning, the end of the twilight, like an unfading star." Still later, addressing the Jewish youth movement, he proclaims, "Your goal is the establishment of a just life. Your enemy is the demon of money, selfishness, trade, and the times in general."

The Eastern Jews in Zweig's account represent not merely individual figures he presumably encountered during his tenure at Ober-Ost, but also something much larger and more mythical. They are types who together symbolize, as Zweig would have us believe, the collective Jewish soul. He thus writes of the cobbler, the homemaker, the Talmud student, and the revolutionary. Moreover, he bolsters the significance of these figures by ascribing to them biblical affinities. The young Jewish girl embodies "our ancestral mother Leah, again at work for the people." Isaac, Jacob, Joseph, Benjamin, and David all find themselves reflected in the Eastern Jews. Or as Zweig puts it, extending the genealogical line, "Israel is a young boy on earth, innocent, disoriented, defiant, and ready to return home if somebody approaches him with the righteous and benevolent word to ease his shame." Finally, near the book's denouement, there is the messianic figure of Abel: "Abel, young Jewish boy, eternal beginning, new spring: one morning, out of the wells of your eyes one shall create the elixir of life. In those Salomon-like mirrors of your eyes, the face of the Messiah shall be reflected, something that has certainly been promised to the people and to the earth, to bring peace and to reveal the goodness of humankind."

The narrative that Zweig artfully constructs gives him the opportunity to infuse the text with various strands of political doctrine and lofty proclamations. As he writes in his opening words, "[I]t is indeed a virtue of humankind and a great inner freedom if one does not participate in the general silence but instead speaks out." And as an act of critical engagement, Zweig includes passages that resemble more of a charged manifesto than a dispassionate commentary:

> These people with their small-minded thoughts from whom
> one always hears the same words, the same intonations—how
> ridiculous they are, how remarkably stupid is their gait! These
> streets, how revoltingly passé, these coffeehouses, how monotonous, these gardens, how dead and how overfilled with wretched
> people! This environment, how foul! A boundless yearning cries
> out: away from here! Into the free air, the vastness, the unknown,
> the freshly created! There is the true life, here merely its phantom;

there is the power, courage, and a wide horizon, here a dead end whose gutter stinks.

Among the central objectives of Zweig's work is the outright rejection of the modern condition. He takes it upon himself, under the guise of defending the Eastern Jews, to let the Western Jews and gentiles alike know that they have gone down the wrong path.

One strategy Zweig employs to accomplish this is to overturn the stereotypes of the Eastern Jew, and of the Jew in general. To discredit the rumor of Eastern Jewish laziness, he writes, "[T]he Jew of the East is ready for work, in handicrafts above all, because in order for him to feel like a living person, he must have a place—and not in an impersonal factory—in which his occupation may be fulfilled. This cobbler who hammers his soles in a tiny workshop, entirely immersed and lost in the fortune of being able to work, that is the true Jew of the East." He similarly weighs in against the stereotype of hypersexuality: "The Jew controls his sexuality; for him, a woman is never merely the personification of a sexual organ, as she is for others, but a human being. Here is a general purity of feeling which has nothing to do with repression." Given Zweig's sympathies for the Socialist cause, which appear to complement his spiritual investment in utopian Zionism, he sees it as his task to discredit the notion of Jewish materialism and rampant greed: the old Eastern Jew, according to Zweig, harbors "contempt for pure money" (which Zweig repeatedly calls "the demon") and "contempt for that which is mere possession." Likewise, he goes to great lengths to demonstrate the import of Socialism among the Eastern Jewish youth: "A burning sense of justice flows in the heart of the youth, of good youth. For to approve of the horrible injustice of the godforsaken life in modern times, to exploit it—a people could not sink much lower than this. And so Jewish youth joins in the outcry for social justice that is called Socialism, and it wants it all."

What, in the end, one might ask, is truly Jewish for Zweig? "Jewish is the Sabbath, Jewish are the holidays and the customary dishes, language, books, ancestors, laws of merit according to which one forms values, and instincts according to which one affirms and negates. Jewish are jokes and gestures, linguistic irregularities and bodily shapes, individual affliction and moral prejudices. All this is Jewish or 'Jewish.'" He remarks further: "Oh people, you strange and glorious people, broken up like after a rain, bursting with sprouts like spring soil—whose heart does not open up with love when he sees you and become inflamed with anger about your essence in the Diaspora?"

As Zweig himself suggests, the crucial advantage of the second edition of *The Face of East European Jewry*—the edition on which the present English translation is based—over the first is the correspondence between text and image. The fifty-two drawings by Struck cover much of the same ground as does Zweig's text, taking the Eastern Jews as occasions for the expression of dignity, tenacity, pride, and hope. Struck intersperses close-up profiles, which reveal not only the rich features of his subjects but also the mastery of his craft, with images of Eastern Jews performing the most prosaic of activities: an old man reading a book; another carrying a sack over his shoulder; a woman writing; a young boy begging. There are only two drawings without human subjects—one of a house of prayer and the other of a Jewish home. In many cases, Zweig gives extended expositions of the images. Take, for instance, his musings on the mother holding her young baby:

> The Jewish woman, with a child in her arms, reveals the most well rounded character of the East. Only the old man, with the Torah scrolls in his arms or holding a book in both hands, is comparable to her. The shawl, draped from her shoulders and wrapped around the small creature, does not cover the child more warmly or more fully than the expression that she casts from beneath her eyelashes. She is, at this point, no longer worthy of adornment herself; her hair, strictly hidden beneath an artificial wig, denies her entire feminine desire to be beautiful. Just as honest and strong as her face is, so too is her concern about this pledge to the future.

Nearly all of Zweig's expositions incorporate both thick description and close analysis of where these figures might fit into Jewish life in the East and what they might represent for humanity.

At times, Zweig's paean to the *Ostjuden* strikes a decidedly patronizing tone not unlike that of cultural anthropological tracts on primitive native tribes. For instance, in his pitched discussion of the conditions of Eastern Jewish living, he notes, "They are poor, they make do without taste, but they are entirely suffused with a hominess that rises about all else." Even a poverty-stricken ghetto existence can appear quaint or cozy to an adoring observer. Along similar lines, he writes of the old Eastern Jewish men: "They appear to be the disinherited, refugees of life, oblivious to the dirt on their clothes and to the common vermin that hardly trouble them anymore." Or, as he reflects on the young Jewish girls, he discovers what he calls "the innocent tranquility, the trusting nature of organic creatures." Zweig is at least tacitly aware of the subjective nature of his work, admitting as he does in the penultimate chapter, "[T]his book is not supported by specialized literature, not by reports, but rather merely by the present condition of life and by the spiritual gift of observing. It is as wrong or right as the configuration itself which life presents to the observer. Hence the gaps, hence the exaggerations: it is a testimony."

Zweig and Struck were certainly not the only German-speaking Jews to witness and chronicle the life of the *Ostjuden*. In fact, a number of prominent Weimar-era writers, most notably Alfred Döblin and Joseph Roth, would subsequently embark upon a "journey to the Jews," as Roth referred to Döblin's *Reise in Polen* (1926; English translation, *Journey to Poland*, 1991).[17] Döblin shared Zweig's sympathetic impression of the Eastern Jews as an unsullied, intact community distinct from Jewish life in the West. "They are a nation," as he put it. "People who know only Western Europe fail to realize this. The Jews have their own costumes, their own language, religion, manners and mores, their ancient national

17. Joseph Roth, "Döblin im Osten," *Frankfurter Zeitung*, 31 January 1926.

feeling and consciousness."[18] Writing a short time after Döblin, in his *Juden auf Wanderschaft* (1927; English translation, *Wandering Jews*, 2001), a series of vignettes on Jewish life, Roth communicated the aims of his book directly to his readers. As he writes in the foreword, "The author has the fond hope that there may still be readers from whom the Eastern Jews do not require protection, readers with respect for pain, for human greatness, and for the squalor that everywhere accompanies misery. . . . These are readers who feel they might have something to learn from the East, and who have perhaps already sensed a great people and great ideas."[19] As in the case of Döblin, and Zweig before him, Roth sets the Eastern Jews apart from their Western brothers and sisters, Jews who, in his words, "gave themselves up" and "became ordinary middle-class people."[20]

No matter how one approaches the book today, *The Face of East European Jewry* is very much a product of its time. It represents a broader trend that swept across Weimar Germany and beyond. It has, in other words, as much to do with the war experience as with the attendant pan-European developments in the literary, cultural, and political sphere. The focus—not to mention the experimental style—of Zweig's writing may be compared to other, non-German works of the period. For instance, the Russian novelist Isaac Babel, in his *1920 Diary*, remarks of the Ukrainian and Galician Jews he encountered on his cavalry tour, "Their faces—this is the ghetto, and we are an ancient people, exhausted, but we still have some strength left. . . . They are like portraits, elongated, silent, long-bearded, not like our type, fat and jovial."[21] Like Zweig, Babel zeroes in on the facial features of his subject, noting their distinc-

18. Alfred Döblin, *Journey to Poland*, trans. Joachim Neugroschel, ed. Heinz Graber (New York: Paragon House, 1991), 50.

19. Joseph Roth, *Wandering Jews*, trans. Michael Hofmann (New York: Norton, 2001), 2.

20. Roth, *Wandering Jews*, 14.

21. Isaac Babel, *1920 Diary*, ed. Carol J. Avins, trans. H. T. Willetts (New Haven: Yale University Press, 1995), 28–29.

tiveness and what separates them from more assimilated Jews who don the uniform of a non-Jewish occupying force. The focus on physiognomy, however, was not limited to writers alone. The realm of the visual arts in general, and photography in particular, showed itself to be equally pre-occupied with the "face of the era," as August Sander called his famous Weimar collection of photographic portraits.[22] Such images, like those by Struck, together form what one astute critic has recently called "a group portrait of an entire nation."[23] They document a specific epoch, a cultural moment, and in doing so, suggest a shared experience.

When it originally appeared, *The Face of East European Jewry* was greeted with mixed reviews. The literary and cultural critic Moritz Gold-stein noted the book's noble statement in favor of "Jewish commonal-ity" and the generally praiseworthy effort it makes to ensure that "East-ern Jewry will always be able to be protected against haughtiness and ignorance."[24] Writing in *Das jüdische Echo*, in a survey of literature on and by Eastern Jews, Alfred Döblin hailed the work for its timeliness (and, considering his later travels to Poland, Döblin himself appears to have taken to heart the example set by Zweig and Struck).[25] In a rather barbed dissent, Paul Zucker, reviewing the book in the pages of Buber's *Der Jude*, likened the work to a "holiday sermon in a Zionist newspaper."[26] For Zucker, both Zweig and Struck were guilty of rendering an overly sen-timental, overly imaginative portrait and of projecting inflated images that he pronounced "Mythen der Gegenwart" (myths of the present).

In a move perhaps anticipated to a certain extent by their joint affirma-tion of life in a utopian Jewish community, both Zweig and Struck would

22. See August Sander, *Antlitz der Zeit* (Munich and Berlin: Transmare Verlag, 1929).

23. John von Hartz, introduction to *August Sander* (New York: Aperture, 1997), 5.

24. Goldstein, "Arnold Zweig," 249.

25. Alfred Döblin, "Alfred Döblin über ostjüdische Dichtung," *Das jüdische Echo* 38 (1924): 285–287.

26. Paul Zucker, "Mythen der Gegenwart," *Der Jude* 7/8 (1924): 465.

eventually leave their native Germany and migrate, making *aliyah,* to Palestine. The more committed Zionist of the two, Struck settled in Haifa in 1923, whereas Zweig left only after the Nazi ascent to power in 1933. Zweig's greatest hour of fame, however, came before he left Germany. His powerful antiwar novel *Der Streit um den Sergeanten Grischa* (1927; English translation, *The Case of Sergeant Grischa*, 1928) drew international attention in the United States and elsewhere; the English translation sold 25,000 copies in the first print run alone.[27] Many of Zweig's writings from around this period, nearly all of them preoccupied with the experience of war, were soon translated into English. Zweig also continued to pursue Jewish matters and concerns up to the point of his emigration: in his second book with Struck, his reflections on the Holy Land, *Das neue Kanaan* (The new Canaan, 1925); his summation of the Jewish contribution to German theater, *Juden auf der deutschen Bühne* (Jews on the German stage, 1927); his Freudian inspired examination of antisemitism, *Caliban oder Politik und Leidenschaft* (Caliban; or, politics and emotion, 1927); his novel based on a scandalous murder case in 1920s Palestine, *De Vriendt kehrt heim* (1932; English translation, *De Vriendt Goes Home*, 1933); and his final reckoning with German Jewry, *Bilanz der deutschen Judenheit* (1933; English translation, *Insulted and Exiled,* 1937).[28] While living in Palestine, Zweig continued to write in German and to maintain strong ties to that cultural world; he published a German-language journal, *Orient*, and refused to adopt Hebrew as his lingua franca. Very soon after Israel's declaration of independent statehood, with his dreams of a utopian Zionism shattered by the war, a disenchanted Zweig returned to the fledg-

27. Arnold Zweig, *The Case of Sergeant Grischa*, trans. Eric Sutton (New York: Viking, 1928).

28. See Arnold Zweig, *Das neue Kanaan: Eine Untersuchung über Land und Geist* (Berlin: Horodisch & Marx, 1925); *Juden auf der deutschen Bühne* (Berlin: Heine-Bund, 1927); *Caliban oder Politik und Leidenschaft* (Berlin: Kiepenheuer, 1927); *De Vriendt Goes Home*, trans. Eric Sutton (New York: Viking, 1933); *Insulted and Exiled: The Truth about German Jews*, trans. Eden and Cedar Paul (London: Miles, 1937).

ling German Democratic Republic, where he felt his literary aspirations and political ideals might be better fulfilled. Still engaged in a delicate balancing act between Zionism, Socialism, and antiwar activism, Zweig died in East Berlin in 1968. During the final years of his life, he was celebrated as a state-sponsored author, while West Germany, and the West in general, paid little heed to his work.

In the afterword to the 1929 reprint of *Das ostjüdische Antlitz*, Zweig poses a question that anticipates the eventual demise of the Eastern Jewish community: "Perhaps we, the generation of the war, were the last ones who were able to observe the old Eastern Jewish face."[29] The world he and Struck witnessed no longer exists. Yet, over eight decades after its original release, *The Face of East European Jewry* may now reach a new generation of English-speaking readers who, perhaps for the first time, will experience at least some of what Zweig hoped for.

A NOTE ON THE TRANSLATION

Translating Zweig's text has not been a straightforward task. It has entailed difficult decisions and many hurdles. Part of what accounts for this is that Zweig's manuscript is, on many counts, a very strange piece of writing. The tone is strange; strange, too, is the structure. Yet rather than attempting to reshape this book into something more akin to a contemporary Anglo-American style—which would, in my estimation, be tantamount to rewriting the work *in toto*—I have tried as best as possible to retain the flavor of the original in the English rendition. This may not always make for the most reader-friendly prose, but it does, I hope, give a stronger sense of the rare quality of Zweig's work.

There are a couple of finer semantic matters worth addressing, if only in passing. Occasionally I have added editorial clarifications to certain German words Zweig uses which I chose to leave in the original for the

29. Arnold Zweig, "Nachwort," *Herkunft und Zukunft: Zwei Essays* (Vienna: Phaidon, 1929), 225.

purpose of historical and cultural nuance, and also to words or phrases requiring minor explication. These interpolations appear in brackets. As for Zweig's inclusion of non-German foreign words, I have attempted in most cases to leave these unchanged, with my English translation appearing in brackets next to the word or phrase; the use of ellipses by Zweig has similarly been left unchanged. *Ostjude* (*Ostjuden* in the plural, *ostjüdisch* as adjective), a term that Zweig employs throughout the work, belonged to common parlance among Weimar-era Germans, Jew and gentile alike, when referring to East European Jews. On occasion I leave the term in the original, without English translation; otherwise, I have rendered it as "Eastern Jew" or "Eastern Jewish." However, the English title of Zweig's work—literally, "The Eastern Jewish Face" or "The Face of Eastern Jewry"—has been given the "European" modifier for the sake of making the focus of the work more comprehensible to today's English-speaking reader. To assist the reader further, I have included a glossary listing brief explanations of some of the names and terms used by Zweig in *The Face of East European Jewry*.

Finally, I would like to express a few words of gratitude: first, to Sheila Levine at the University of California Press for her determination, even when there were numerous signs that the project might not reach the light of day; to Maria Pelikan, who served as a valuable and persistent liaison to the German publishing world; to Steven Aschheim and John Efron for their instructive readers' reports; and last but not least, to Edward Dimendberg for his fervent support from the very outset, and to his colleagues in the Weimar and Now series, Martin Jay and Anton Kaes, who similarly took great interest in shepherding this work toward its final completion.

Noah Isenberg
New York City
August 2003

PREFACE TO THE SECOND EDITION

This book, which poured forth out of a passion and out of a specific intent, was nonetheless accepted and completed at an inauspicious time for the soul—it is a book that had to be released from me more quickly than expected. Today, as I read through it again, the very "what" of its expression, as well as its "how," no longer agrees with me. Because I couldn't change the first—it was not objective reasons but rather a generally more sober spirit of life which prevailed against that—I have only changed the second, reconciling that which was averse to the pathos-laden and solemn manner of expression—carefully and with deference to the original book released from me. Only philology may detect the changes—and hopefully the ear of the good reader. This edition has one advantage over the first: the correspondence of text and image. In this regard, it expresses more plainly the intention of our collaboration, and as a result it is—at least in my opinion—far superior to the other edition.

At this point, the fact that there lies before us, within this apologetic work, a work that has made its main object the world of a people, the first provisional sign of a human transformation of the author cannot be concealed. He is not a poet—even the most personal matters of the author, a writer of epics and dramas, have to be revealed in objective terms.

And here another word about the preface: Poland long ago proved itself to be a cultured nation *[Kulturland]*, at least since the cases of Hungary and the Ukraine, in whose atrocious pogroms the dregs of militaristic baseness have now been brought to light.

Not a word can be said to offset the crimes committed against the Jews there. They don't whitewash Poland, but after all one tends to no longer pay attention to the murders and crimes committed in a country it once governed. Hungary and the Ukraine have proven that their heroes were far more energetic and inventive, far wiser and more thorough in taking action against the lives of unarmed Jews than were their Polish counterparts, who were no amateurs themselves.

And yet, Europe, preoccupied with the exploitation of the victors of Versailles, was not able to concern itself with this, the one and only glorious exception being the English Socialists, whose Colonel Wedgewood went there, observed, and reported endlessly to the House of Commons on all the atrocities he witnessed. He was commissioned to do so by his party, which when considered today in terms of its humanity, fought at the forefront of the true European spirit.

Today it is indeed a virtue of humankind and a great inner freedom if one does not participate in the general silence but instead speaks out.

Starnberg, Spring 1922
A. Z.

PREFACE TO THE FIRST EDITION

This book about the Eastern Jews is written by somebody who has attempted to observe them. During the days in which the plan for a book came into being—a year ago, in a Lithuanian Jewish city—one might have expected much concerning the fate of our brothers, none of it trivial. For it appeared then as if the anti-Jewish hands of the Prussian military and financial guardians would continue to linger like a shadowy cloud over the East. And, indeed, we thought that alone would be very bad.

But what in fact came was the rule of plunder, of whips and clubs, executions and murders, disappearances without a trace and rotting away in prisons. Alas, we did not anticipate the wrath of the Poles.

We spoke with our brothers and sisters while still dressed in the uniform of the German soldiers. They said, "Your regime is disgusting. You control and harass by use of power, you beat innocent human beings during interrogations, you confiscate and steal, and you insult us with your contempt. Your battalions of slave laborers are like having a kind of Siberia in the middle of our own country; your decrees aim at allowing the weak to die from starvation and epidemics which weren't here before. It was better under the czar than under you—if only the Russians would return! And yet, we'll get along with the Lithuanians and the White Russians, and even with you. Just don't leave us to the Poles, for then all of us are doomed."

Poles and pogroms have descended upon the Eastern Jewish people, who live one on top of the other in the big cities and who are also scattered about the villages and small towns. Devastating news comes from the big cities, while the villages and small towns, those without railroads and without telegraph, remain silent. Slowly one hears what's happening there: either murder or massacre.

I don't believe a single word of all the denials that are now being composed, disseminated, or put forth by the governing rule of Poland. One needs merely to have spent two months in Lithuania to think as I do with such urgent conviction.

The Jews of the East want to live in their own Jewish way, in their own cultural milieu, with their own beliefs and their own languages. Like Dutch or English, Yiddish is a language in and of itself—something that the Polish assimilationists would of course scornfully dispute.

I know that there exist refined and intelligent Poles. Unfortunately, however, they can't bring our brothers back to life.

We attribute this murder and suffering to the people of Poland, so that even the better ones should turn red with shame when they see a Jew. For it is not a matter of being better, but rather of putting an end to it. And for that, they are too few and too weak.

We say here and now what Europe and America could also say today, if it weren't for their deeply crazed anxiety concerning every form of Socialism: the murdered Jews, so far as they were Socialists at all, were not murdered on account of their "Bolshevism."

To begin the futile battle against Socialism justifiably in one's own home and to lead with convincing moral lessons and edifying deeds—is that too much to expect? Perhaps it is today, when Europe, excited by the scent of blood and an obsession with killing, dashes wildly down the path that leads to the destruction and overturning of an era.

Thus, for the Poles we predict that the Polish people themselves will avenge our brothers: by way of Polish Socialism.

May Israel think of the crimes of Poland as the crimes of Amalek, who today, even after three thousand years, is not forgiven for having brought to our brothers countless murders—the disasters of epidemics, of war and starvation, genocide, and the cowardly murder of the defenseless by the armed.

Of course, we were unable to rush to your aid. And each word that we speak for you will be regarded, by those who could help, as dirty lies and German politics.

You died as a result of a cowardly, murderous, profit-hungry phase in Europe. What good does it do that later generations will be ashamed for the sake of your murdered souls? That's all entirely in vain.

At least the testimony of a human being does not die. And so we bear witness for you, and we leave it up to our perceptive readers to discern when only one of us speaks and when it is both of us.

May the taste of blood upon the tongue of the man-eating bull that is Europe soon disappear.

"Do you believe that I take pleasure in the death of the godless," speaks the Lord. "Or rather, that he is transformed from his essence and he lives?"

Summer 1919
In the month of Ab 5679
Arnold Zweig   Hermann Struck

I.

He turns his eye away from me and into the distance, a distance that is nothing but time. His profile leads like a waterfall into his beard, which dissolves into spray and clouds. The nobility of his posture and his nose, the spirituality of his pensive and furrowed brow, contrast the hard, defiant ear and meet in his gaze, a gaze that neither demands nor renounces, neither longs for nor laments what it is. And his gaze draws upon itself a distance about which we know that it is nothing but time.

Is this the Jew of the East? Is he an old man, who, almost entirely removed from the present day and certainly removed from the future, lives a life that is limited to the most oppressed and narrowest form, a life that scatters once the pressure that forced it into that form is relieved? We know that our forefathers were relatives of the men we find today in the cities of Lithuania, Poland, and Galicia; no, we know that they lived in the Franconian hill regions and the German plains like us. Thus, today we speak different languages, think different thoughts, live a different kind of Judaism, eat different dishes, measure according to different standards, and we have traded part of our soul with Europe, giving up part of our Jewishness. For nearly five generations it has shaped us, this European fate and its freedom, its new air, its wonderful and artistic values, its integrating and liberating aura. And then it took the most explicit crisis of all to bring us to our senses: crisis of the heart, crisis of memory, crisis of countenance *[Antlitz]*. For it is out of the stern, modest, forward-turned face of the Jew—the witness to the indolence of our times and to the mightiness of a willfully chosen national substance—that the bloated, transparent, and flat caricature of the Jewish trader on Nordic terrain is made, destined to disappear in the muck of eternal "newness" *[Jetztzeit]* in all big cities.

The Jew of the West was on his way toward a kind of ossified denomination, toward an eviscerating, desperate piety which cut itself off from all tradition and was incapable of doing anything but cutting itself off. Due to fervent atheism and an exaggerated and totally false application of scientific objectivity, this denomination was declining from day to day, crumbling away, losing weight faster and faster, and in front of his own eyes, as if automatically and without resistance, the Jew of the West left these obvious losses to the mercy of the disaster. The youth first traveled the path toward Europe—which is the code name for a pleasure-filled, functional, absolutely modern metropolis—secretly, then openly, first hesitantly and then defiantly, immodestly, and finally, in a kind of deliberate casualness. They traveled the path to Europe, the alluring, rose-covered, enlightened path of a cultural decline into mishmash.

The old Jew of the East, however, preserved his face. It looks at us from the tales of Mendele [Moykher Sforim, i.e., Shalom Abramovitch], this face: sincere and dreamy and of a purity which can be procured only at the cost of sacrificing one's broader activities and the happiness of broader activity. To start a small trade, to eat bread and herring, to father and raise children, to say the daily prayers and the prayers over meals, and to read many pages of Gemara; to give a bit to the poor from the little that one earns, to provide daughters for marriage, to visit the sick, to bury the dead, and to console the mourners—this is the pattern of his duties, and how effortlessly he bears it upon himself. As he is of a young and cheerful heart, he is not paralyzed by the search for a livelihood, which is only then made possible through a spiritual turn toward money as that

which has the highest value—and he refuses to make this turn. As he has a young and cheerful heart, the heart of a lifelong pupil who knows about the imperfection of knowledge and about the noble, unspoken happiness of honoring great teachers, the happiness of duty and its natural spirit continue to pour out of him.

His alert, stoic eyes and his mouth, which conveys his great kindness and hides delicately behind his beard, together testify that here the naturalness and levity of all obligations still prevail. Here duty is not something forced or weighed with an exact scale, nor is it that which is shamelessly bestowed upon the community as the minimum amount of work. It is not that which gave life in the West its empty, barren, and foul-tasting concept of duty, so that it became sensible to say, "Do more than your duty, if something good should be achieved." To the Jew of the East, duty is "the order of the day" and its fulfillment pours so guilelessly and perfectly out of the most fundamental nature of his heart that he would stand just as uncomprehendingly before the words "more than your duty" as he would before any groaning about one's duty, groaning that lends these words their oiliness and ugliness. He conducts himself with the composure of an innocent human being, and the mark of his cap, which seldom leaves his head, is no more common in his hand than is his conduct commonly unmediated to the point of laughter.

Nothing is lovelier than the untiring cheerfulness of the Jew. Even if old age and the travails of life have rendered his head bald, left wrinkles in his forehead, carved deep folds beneath his eyes, and molded his cheeks like those of a woodcut—precisely there, in the corner of his taut mouth, on his nose, and around his eyes, lies a transgression that triumphs. It triumphs: over what? Over fear? But nothing is more foreign to the Eastern Jew than the constant feeling of being threatened, the need at least to worry about his well-being if not to fight for it. For God, before whose eyes he continually lives, is a father, and his knowledge of the frail soul of the human being is just as large as his gracious sense of righteousness and love, which flows from his fatherly heart. To be loved by this immediate God, in a strict and fatherly manner, to stand before him with

all his actions revealed, and to welcome, with deep conviction, his punishment as well as his kindness—that is the manner of the Eastern Jew before God.

Nobody is able to stand before the Lord more naturally than the Jew who enters the house of the eternal one, this small expanse of earth surrounded by walls covered with stones and modestly decorated. There is no trace of reverence in the room, no glorification of eternity or justice fills him, no yearning arches pull him closer to heaven, no sepulcher weighs the yoke of his fallibility heavily upon his neck. There are no signposts that remind him that he may have lost his way in the forest of mortal pretense and that only once he's found his way out of the mortally dangerous dawning of this petrified forest might the true life, the life of the next world, lie before him like a brilliant valley at sunrise, filled with larks chirping and the fresh air of the Sabbath. No, there is no fear of God here, no holy ground. Rather, this is a house for human beings— and reverence, quivering, yearning, and the weight of fallibility are all together in the prayer that at times makes the room swing like the pendulum of a breathing soul. Over what does this transgression triumph? Over the yoke of human life. The Jew is more harshly afflicted than scarcely any other people or class on earth.

For the climate of an Indian or Chinese summer does not help him avoid the worries about finding a home, even if his living costs are otherwise close to being the handful of rice with which the slave or pariah must renew his strength. Still, in the face of such a spiritual rigor mortis— which, for the European worker of all hostile eras, obscures the horizon of spiritual values and forces him to see in his children nothing more than the continuation of his own oppressed proletarian slave existence—he is generally able to save himself. Even the benefit of being able to regard oneself as a struggling member of a more humane caste or class, dispersed throughout the world, is in the broadest sense lost on him, because he was born with an indescribably poor, though petit bourgeois and non-proletarian, goal of existence. [They are] piled upon each other in an environment whose tumultuous confinement may only be illustrated by comparison to aquariums in fancy restaurants, in which so many fish are squeezed between narrow glass walls that they are barely covered by water, that very vital and indispensable element. Moreover, the fish are stacked and pressed against the transparent, obstinate barrier either with their mouths clinging to the surface of the aquarium or pinned to the sandy bottom. The Jews are crowded together not all that differently in the shtetls or large cities of the East. One Jew barely distinguished from the next—smalltime trader, craftsman, skilled or itinerant worker, coachman, water carrier, messenger, broker—all equal to one another in their pursuit of their own household affairs, in their vision of themselves with wife and children in possession of their own kitchen, whose stove gives each Jew the dignity of the *Baal Habayit*, the so-called Balbos, the head of the household.

The struggle for one's existence, which has to be fought for the sake of kopeks or pfennigs, is not led by the united front of a union. For in fact it was not proletarian workers who needed to fight, but the petite bourgeoisie—each of them living cramped next to, and at the same time far from, the other, and each, in his individualistic ideal, making up a social circle—it is they who are the most difficult to unite and almost impossible to organize. Each one like the other, and yet through the nuance of all others different, as each emphasizes with severity his own nuance: they are Jews! And as such, each sacrifices wrongheadedly the possibility of rising to a better position by way of collective bargaining, because each sees in it a concession in which he should sacrifice the irrevocable individuality of his being.

From the protective brim of his cap and the shield of his upturned collar—his exposed mouth covered by his beard—the experienced and tested son of an age-old people allows only his objective, watchful eye and his poised nose to be seen. He is like a wise old badger being hunted, and yet like a greenhorn, he carries his home around with him. Thus, reserved, well-kept, not at all suspicious or mistrustful but without the obviousness of an all-too-common premature enthusiasm, he confronts life, whose extremities he knows well. It is the sense of reality of a veteran

that appears to be embodied in him, that is part of this son of the earth as it is, like the sense of reality of a farmer who without allowing himself to be demoralized is able to deduce from the seasons, from the good and the wicked weather, the next harvest. It is the sense of reality of a wise old man that appears to be the clearest folk expression of the Jew, which is appropriate given the age of the nation he represents. And this very folk tradition itself, steadfastly preserved in language, dress, customs, and spirituality, as adopted from the fourteenth or fifteenth century and altered only superficially, appears to be as immutable and tenacious as an old man who is not threatened by illness. And so, would not resignation and the inability to revive the old man be the deepest and most incriminating expression of the Eastern Jew, of the Jew in general? Sometimes one gets the sense that one cannot avoid this conclusion.

A noble and silent beauty of the evening lies upon his forehead. His deep-set eyes, resting softly, like dusky ponds, in the shadows of his chiseled cheekbones, know much wisdom but no longer blink at action. The tenderness of his mouth speaks in the words of the preacher about our vanity and about our chasing after the wind of our transitory existence. The composure of such human beings is startling; they saunter through the lower depths and with them the throngs of the forefathers, who, like them, have eaten from the bitter bread of exile and externally imposed misery. They have no sense of hopelessness or of the severity of despair in them, not even disillusionment. So closely related to rebellion and to the cry of death is their fate, in which timidity affirms itself. Their hope and outlook are invested in the will of God, who will bring redemption during his reign. However, as a result, each revolt and each step toward auto-emancipation cuts itself off, like a river flowing endlessly toward a horizon, silently and irrevocably cutting the lowlands in two. The will of God: that is the horizon of the Jew—not a gaping black hole, not a mountain range poised to emerge, but rather the faintly trembling line of the marriage between heaven and earth. It would require prophetic words to describe how little of the poison that is called fatalism is in this soulful peace. For to build bridges to the will of God, to be for him the

means of fulfillment, is left up to the Jew, and indeed, this is the purpose of his life.

In this regard, the grand Eastern Jewish creation of Hasidism pours into the most prosaic of daily activities, into the most immediate call of the day. Whoever lives simply in the proximity of such matters and such people, whoever protects his soul from giving in to breathless futility, whoever provides lovingly and openly each movement of his hands, each word of his mouth, and whoever gives each connection to his fellow human being and to those brotherly creations a ray of warmth and a friendly heart: he partakes of the redemption of the providence of humankind, which since the beginning of time has been deeply rooted in the providence of the Jew. This great, mature benevolence, the peaceful sincerity of each hour, is commonly visible with profound gentleness among the old Eastern Jews. And sometimes, as one eventually recognizes, they are Hasidim who stand, like ripened pear trees, at the center of the lush, flourishing field of everyday life. And is it not a kind of true participation in the coming redemption, when peace and benevolence fall onto the violent, thrashing hustle and bustle of human life like pears falling onto windswept grass? Are not liberation and celebration here, when the quarreling surrounding such an old man subsides, when the never-ending market is forgotten and the never-ending hunt must be silent? When nervous gestures wear off, violent and loud voices become silent, and as a result of the friendly encouragement of his knowledge much reveals itself as unimportant, in particular that which erected the fences of animosity between human beings? Just how strongly the Eastern Jewish people *[Volk]* allows itself to be bound by such old men can be seen in the dramas of its theater. Quite often, in the last act, when nobody else wants to get caught in the thick plot of human and masculine limitation, the Zeyde, the grandfather—up until then treated merely as a wise spare piece of obscure equipment—produces his resolving power: partly because of his conviction, partly because of the dignity of his being, the serenity of his wisdom prevails as he offers everything toward the good and toward the heart-warming. And he then stands at the center of that which he has offered, like a god in a Greek drama or a Shakespearean duke, dressed in the natural and cheerful appearance of every human being to whom unconstrained inner obedience is owed.

What if after such a hard life, after the unending struggle for a little bread for man, wife, and children, cheerfulness of this sort represents the end—must not there be a kind of substance in each human being which keeps him from allowing degradations to touch the core of his soul? For there is often still suffering from apparent and real degradations, even where Jew and Jew work side by side. Money leads Jew and non-Jew alike toward a trifling and wretched upward mobility; the more sickly are not spared the sickening words and he, if he has listened to how the Polish lord or the German officer, for whom the Jew clearly represents the weaker of the two, speaks to the Jew, could keep the consternation far from himself. But if one guesses from his big, open eyes, which, motionless under the curved eyebrows, look at the symbol of upward mobility, does one suspect the tension of a strained smile, which dives down from the nostrils of his expressive nose into the tangle of his beard? The intention of degradation passes right by him, falling down into the patient and silent earth, which is stepped upon but not degraded. What this height of being bestows upon the old Jew, what makes him untouchable, is his contempt for pure money. The contempt for that which is mere possession. The contempt for being obsessed with rather than uninterested in possession. The great contempt that the noble spirit possesses against the demon—without the self-possession of the spirit.

The large rugged ear of the poor man does not hear irony, ranting, or insult, for it has fully absorbed the melody muttered in the evening, after the trials and tribulations of the day, the melody he hums while poring over pages of Gemara in the house of study. His bony forehead cannot hide its searching, for still circulating behind it are questions about the true meaning of an expression during the interpretation of which, in the urgent exercise of argument and counterargument on the true opinion of the great teacher, the candles burned out last night. Learning: learning which lasts a lifetime, learning whose purpose is the unceasing

devotion of one's entire body and all human power to its lessons, learning gives the simple Jew the unassailable quality of his being. And the
boundlessness of the endeavor protects itself against arrogance, which is
an impediment to the spiritual.

There is no championship here, for the gravity of the Talmud and its
attendant task is eternal. Here there are those who are developing as well
as those who are advanced, beginners and older comrades, but there is
no single "initiate," no single "perfect" one, no single "righteous" one.
For the Jew, even today, the spiritual human being represents the pinna-
cle of all human beings. To choose a poor son-in-law because he is a
Lamed, somebody who is renowned in learning, is still the best "catch"
for the small-town Jew. It's entirely true that as a result of the war, wealth
has gained respect, and that morality has suffered in the face of this. Yet
no rich man—so long as he wishes to be counted among those living with
the people at all—can deem himself to be positioned higher above the
incorruptible feeling of the people than he who lives in accordance with
the law and learning. The spell cast upon traders, whose shady deals and
haggling threaten the sustenance of the people, has still been the most
effective weapon of the capitalist spirit, which, without looking right or
left, merely chases after surplus value.

Yet the upstanding Eastern Jew also knows irreverence: namely,
toward all that power and the rule of power are or what they attempt to
be. Especially when faced with a violent state, he is incapable of sum-
moning up reverence, respect, or other feelings that recognize the state,
exalt it, or promote it highly. Eastern Jews wander through the streets,
men with their hunched shoulders, long coats, twirled side-locks in front
of their ears, beards without which one cannot imagine them, and their
calm eyes. They appear to be the disinherited, refugees of life, oblivious
to the dirt on their clothes and to the common vermin that hardly trouble them anymore. Work is no longer of much value to their hands, as
they do not invest much hope in great earnings. They do not acknowledge the foreign oppressive state, neither the idols and powerful body of
the West nor the Tartar-dominated Russian East. The state does not have

even the most limited permanence in their minds; it does not exist in their world. Yet they are not revolutionaries. How should they continue to invoke spite, indignation, or rebellion after such a long life? Moreover, how can one experience spite, indignation, rebellion toward such a recent phenomenon as the antidemocratic state? (However, they are the parents of revolutionaries.)

For around four centuries, or around two millennia, these men with their hunched shoulders have been ruled by foreign and brutal states. They have felt only the absurdity, the violence, the oppressive rule by fist as directed toward themselves. And they have thoroughly despised these feelings, so deeply despised them that this contempt is no longer a maxim but rather the bedrock itself of all feelings which the sight of the state elicits in them. These foreigners, these non-Jews who have replaced reasonable, persuasive, and convincing rules of conduct with a sweating, crunching, eye-rolling robot! Without violent oppression, without armed command, they don't know how to get along with human beings! They enslave and they enslave, and they expect that a free Jew should intrinsically recognize, respect, and comply with his enslavement! Add to this a dumb policeman, a bigoted bureaucrat, a regimented soldier, an officer who is drunk on his own power—one with company eyes and a career brain equipped with an obsession with rank—all of whom have the essential needs to regulate and dictate the desires and passions of living human beings and to back them into a corner with punishment or threats of punishment!

And when might this state have ever shown the Jews fairness and friendliness? Not since the days of the great Polish kings, and just as little before then. Wherever a state treated the Jew loyally and honestly, he compensated the state with honesty and loyalty until his death. From the time of the Jews who defended Alexander's cities and those who fought alongside the Goths of Theoderich on the embankments of Naples against the Byzantines, up to the time of those who fought voluntarily in the Polish revolts and all those dead Jews of the world war, they never capitulated in the face of violence. And so, even where the Jew isn't guaranteed a raw, pure human life, where he abandons every bit of the rage of the underlings to pillage with chilling satisfaction, they deal with him like they deal with an extremely dumb, big-mouthed beast. They despise him and they deceive him, if one can really call it deception, which is merely evasion of annoying, nonsensical, and outrageous regulations. For one can only deceive somebody whose right one acknowledges even though—and insofar as—one evades it. The Jews have their own regulations, laws, and directives, which are valid for them and which they do not evade, and which the subjugating state places in opposition to them. For them, it is a meaningless, nonexistent, formal mode of being, to which corruption—disrespect and willful ignorance—is the only appropriate response of the superior and the cunning.

And so would they then be atoms and swarms of atoms, these Jews of the East, incapable of forming a living society of human beings, one founded on the unity of giving and receiving, of procreation and exchange, of invention and experience? Whoever believes this judges all too hastily. The Eastern Jew disavows the oppressive state—the Roman conception of the state—because he lives in a vital folk community *[Volksgemeinschaft]*, because he recognizes the infinitely bloodier existing form of society building *[Gesellschaftung]* as the brutal, order-based, authoritarian state that it is. The poor man whose hand, marked by grief and resolve, grasps the community charity box and holds it timidly, while his sorrowful and trusting eye examines the giver and feels the amount of compassion contained in the donation—he is the most visible expression of this kind of community. The voluntary nature of this service, that which in principle first enables every kind of communal service, makes it morally honorable, makes it estimable. It is the complete absence of any social constraint; the responsibility of one human being for the other, which gives each demand on the other a legitimacy felt by both; the solidarity in the rhythm of existence, in the perspective of the world, in the judgment of and the openness toward values, in the hierarchy of values; and, finally, the tacit and natural agreement that life is changing and unsteady, but God and that which should be are eternal and unchanging,

that today's person who gives can be, and will be, tomorrow's person who receives, and that fortune is not an honor and misfortune, not a sin. Such instincts, such primal urges, provide the seeds that blossom into a community, which today by no means stands purely and pleasantly cultivated before us, yet which, in terms of opportunity and structure, speaks in a way of living next to and living with the Eastern Jews.

Even in the face of adversity, when one occasionally yells at the other, even in the act of cursing, when one shouts at the other, the acknowledgment must be made: you are blood from my blood. But every action done in accordance with the Jewish moral law of loving kindness and righteous candor, or in the presence of a non-Jew, makes the Eastern Jew into "the Jew" to whomever he acts as he should act among members of the community—and every action that leads him into the gutter, that defames Judaism, this makes the Eastern Jew into "the foreigner," "the non-Jew," with whom one may get into a quarrel over how one deals with those who are hostile. That's why the assimilated, violence-worshiping German Jew is a foreigner and an adversary to the Eastern Jew, and that's why, during the wartime occupation, the gracious and humane German gentile was so often for him "one of his own," a communal brother *[Gemeinschaftsbruder]*. And that's why one might wish to listen closely to the conflicting reports, cheerful and grim alike, that come from the Germans and portray their experiences, joyful or incensed, with the Eastern Jews—and amid these reports to recognize the speaker more than the so often accused. For it is not blood that is the almighty asset and binding agent of such communality, but rather spirit, which may be transported in blood but also transcends blood. "God shall help," says the Jew confidently where the son of Western peoples despairingly experiences God's diminishment or fights like a titan against his fate. That doesn't mean—as it does to the observant Christian—"a miracle shall occur," but rather, "Jews will help," "brothers will help." And the necessary response to this sentence is another sentence heard just as often: "Because we are indeed Jews." . . . Yes, we are members of a community, blood brothers and spiritual brothers, and from mutual support a people grows, while from folk traditions *[Volkstum]* brotherly support grows. Blood and spirit: humane existence, a life that is lived to the fullest.

Inconspicuous and serene is the way of the Eastern Jewish community, an ordinary life that characterizes itself, a life that is lived to the fullest; it is an everyday life, which one encounters with piercing, bright eyes, a face full of wrinkles, and lips firmly sealed—there is, incidentally, always a pipe between the Eastern Jew's teeth. The human being must live and not allow others to live for him, and the experience of many failures, successes, and half-successes teaches that half-failures are the most common. Yet what strength it gives the Jew who knows in the final moment, at the end of his life, that nothing can be done on his behalf; how straightforward and surely estimable his eyes look vis-à-vis the unmovable eyes of life! He would not be a Jew if this last unassailable quality did not give him an indefatigable élan, he would not be a Jew if he were not to sink into essential silence and allow things to happen for him according to the will of life. He lives, he begins each day with an activity of his own, and in his good spirits he senses the presence of God; he is active, with a forward and upward motion of the will to live, he feels the marching rhythm of many of his songs circulating in the pulse of his blood. Nothing feverishly inflamed and nothing quickly extinguished brings him to fits of joy and despair. Rather, the toughness of the old, experienced, gray-haired veteran of the battle of life lifts himself once again, after each blow, back onto his feet. At the age of sixty, even at seventy, he is still capable of trying his luck again, and just as he sticks passionately and firmly to the place that saw him grow old, so too he listens closely and willingly to see if the calling reaches him to follow a new fate. That's why he, who is otherwise connected to old customs, is capable, like no other kind of human being, of maintaining his readiness for this calling—as soon as it hits his core—to express the concern of his people: he is indeed capable of experiencing the power of the national and Zionist ideology.

He knows how to exert so many forms of resistance: the old Jew, the man of the people, has just now worked out for himself the meaning of

the appeal for a Jewish homeland in Canaan, because it merely expressed in a new political form what he always knew: that this land was his land. Yet the old Jew of the East did not see in Herzl's message a utopia, as the Western Jew did, but rather, he recognized with passionate agreement the real, the actual, the indisputable and natural essence of it. And that is why the constituency of supporters of the Zionist cause is much larger than the constituency of Eastern Zionists, from whom the average Jew distinguishes himself with regard to the choice of language and present-day practices. He rejects seeing anything real in an organization, and he reluctantly decides to carry out the groundwork; the journey alone, the act of going there, the acquisition of land, is enough for him. When the people call, he will be ready. But up until then, should one lecture? Hold meetings? Cheer oneself on? For what? One has better things to do, the times are hard, one has to live and earn money for the next day . . . It is enough for him that the idea is there, that it is awake and will be watched after by those who also submitted to it in the form of an organization. They can count on him for the day of action, for he is the son of the people, one who doesn't forget his duties . . . This is how he lives with ideas and Jewish ideas live in him and through him. That is not to say that he should be without exception a nobleman and a purely pious one. The strain of the centuries has oppressed and darkened him; even in this community, as in every community, there are dishonest and greedy, vain and ostentatious, dastardly and depraved people—drinkers (seldom) and gamblers (more frequently), those who are self-righteous and buffoons and dealers completely hardened by their possessions. And it remains certain that in each of them—in the profiteer and the pimp, the bordello owner and the groveling flatterer of the rich and famous, in the show-off and the traitor—there is a lawless unity of nature, a persistence toward the bad, which is far removed from sickly degeneration and discoloration.

It is also certain that nothing can guarantee that one day a calling to reform oneself might not reach this wild heart and burn up the old nature entirely, and a new heart in a new body would be created. And finally, it is certain that the Jew forsakes respect for human life and fear of violence and blood less frequently than anybody else. One may wish to claim that it is cowardice that makes him shy away from the murderer's trap; that is a very superficial observation. What is this cowardice other than the most exaggerated and corrupt form of a primal instinct: Thou shalt not kill, because the soul lives on in one's blood and because spilled blood cannot be repaired by anything. Through the goodness of other human beings there can still be healing of that which the criminal has done to the exploited, to the trafficked and violated girl. All human beings are accomplices before God and are called to atone. The dead man, however, is dead, and the death of the killer is not capable of removing the burden of sin, not a grain of it; even if changing one's ways, repentance, atonement, the cry of remorse, self-indictment, and self-condemnation help cleanse the murderer, it remains that the dead man has been brought to the end of his life and the completion of his mission—there's no doubt about that.

And so we turn our eyes away from this underworld and backdrop, which is not capable of undermining the community of which the Eastern Jew, with all his being, is a part, for he himself is not devalued by it. Time and again he raises his sorrowful eye out of the depths of affliction, his great hope glimmering in the stars of the blackened night sky: the hope for eternity. The weakest of all triumphs over the strongest; with the heroic patience of the old Jew, he knows that the composed passivity of his courage must be stronger than the violent act that undeveloped and rapacious people inflict on him now and then—those who bestow upon his white beard an incriminating honor, even if the same beard is red from the blood of the murdered Jew who lies trampled upon in the filth of an Eastern alleyway. Even then. Again yesterday, as now and then, we read, in the bloodied pages of the history of this people, that cowardly Ukrainian and Polish soldiers, in acts of brutality and debasement, murdered and violated Eastern Jews—human beings who did not defend themselves. Shattered by the purity of such deaths, we all suspect the gesture with which our martyrs allow themselves to be wrapped in the white-striped prayer shawl and to be struck, because they belong to this people

that is at once chosen and downtrodden. They may have wailed under the whips of the beasts, they may have writhed under their boots: they are martyrs of the nation and thus live all the more purely in its memory. The people that does not defend itself will finally triumph. The people that does not defend itself will not disappear. It will not be destroyed. It will survive the current bestial nation, just as it has survived others. And we will not forget anything; the people will not forget anything. Judah is eternal and Amalek, who massacred the weak who did not defend themselves, is merely long-lived. Should he rise up in a shameful time, his eye will always catch sight of the shimmering hair, the pure, thoughtful forehead, and the raised eye of the Jew, and he, Cain-Amalek, formerly a Roman and a German, now a Romanian, a Hungarian, a Ukrainian and Pole, will spill the blood of the Jew, and in that he will find his defeat, his sin, his final death. The Jew is eternal, for the spiritual human being is eternal, and Amalek, the rapacious, cowardly, violent worm, is ephemeral, for one human being grows into the next. Old man, security flows into you from the stars; old man in your prayer shawl, your blood, spilled for all of us, for the defenselessness of the human being, you will rise up again transformed and color the red dawn of the times now and then; you will lead and strengthen the dawning, the end of the twilight, like an unfading star.

Do such feelings lie? Was delusion poured into such conviction? The eyes of the Eastern Jew look at us searchingly. They rest there implacably, wide-set and as firmly fixed in the flowing clouds of his white beard as the stars of Jacob's measuring stick. The wrinkle above his peasant nose is sharp and vertical like the wrinkle in the face of a sailor who covers his eyebrows with his hand in order to see more clearly, like the wrinkle of a painter who foresees the vital character of that which is peering out opposite of him. The sense of reality that gave this part of the Jewish people a concentrated, realist writing style, the call for truth, which it extols, looks out from this judicious face and objects to all that has been said about the Jew of the East. Is what has been said up until now also true? Does he measure up to his life, to the test of the closely shared experience

among the people? Is what has been said not perhaps a well-intended illusion about entirely different existing facts? Perhaps only eloquent rhetoric and an exultant tone covering a masked non-truth? Is the Jew of the East perhaps really an old man at the end of a long life, unable to be rejuvenated or to be born again, standing before his imperceptible death? Is this last part of the Jewish people merely held together as a unified people by the ghetto and condemned to drift apart as soon as the iron bonds are crushed by revolutions and a more peaceful movement has begun? Condemned to atomization, to loss in each individual Jew, like the Jews of the West, each of whom has suffered a loss in Jewishness? Condemned to assimilation, to "modernity," to "newness" *[Jetztzeit]*, to Europe, to mishmash?

And who vouches for the fact that it won't happen so nicely, when it happens? Who dares to speak, and with what right, of the eternity of a people which has been a pariah people almost since the beginning of its existence, a people with which others did not deign to mix and which, when prejudice against the caste—and the curse of the caste—was put aside by the progress of Enlightenment, was ready to enter eagerly into the marriage of all peoples? Who claims to express the eternal mission of a people for whom perhaps merely the reversal of the resentment- and pariah-based value system has made the despised into the one who despises, the excluded into the one who decides who to exclude, the disowned and the one who is at home nowhere into the eternal living and the teacher of humankind? Hasn't there begun in every country from the West onward a kind of de-Jewification *[Entjudung]* of the Jews, which only found its limit in the indignation of the local people, and often not even in that? And what will become of this eternal people if the hot revolutionary air causes the old ethnic glaciers to melt away—will there still remain this Eastern Jewry in its ethnic richness and authenticity? For this is the last part of the Jewish people on earth which has created its own new songs and dances, rituals and myths, languages and forms of community *[Gemeinschaftsformen]*—and which continues to keep them alive and at the same time vigorously preserves the old traditions in all their validity. If the Eastern Jew is an old man who, in his departure, has been transformed by purity, brightness, and wisdom, then the existence of Judaism is only guaranteed as long as other groups of people distinguish themselves, through arrogance and cruelty, from it; and this remaining Eastern Jewry—beautiful, humane, autumnal—is the rose- and violet-colored, golden sunset of the Jewish people. Is the Eastern Jew this old man? We will have to search for the answer.

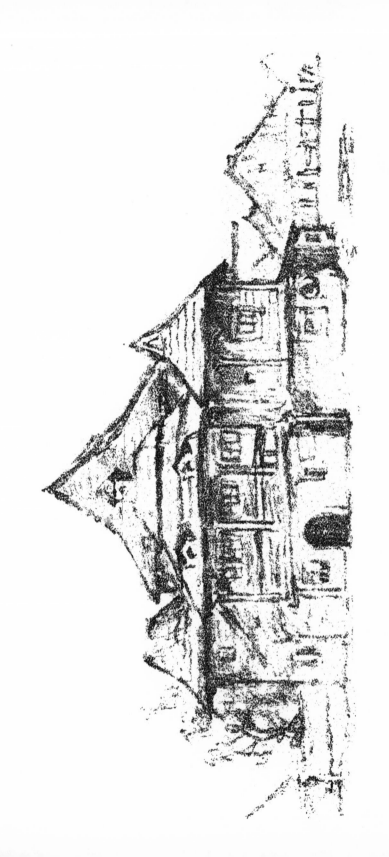

II.

Gray and green, in the natural tones of weathered wooden boards, the houses of worship stand—like this one, on hilly streets or in a valley, in the middle of a village or in an outlying town, almost in the open air—with their pointed roofs, whose non-ornamental and naturally beautiful curves have so much authentic expression, organized and varied, plain and composed like the soul of the human being that should blossom inside. The house's thin columns of smoothed beams are like nuances, the small windows and the lowered door, at human height, are those of a homestead. Old trees are always nearby, as are the modest wooden huts of simple Jews whose lives revolve around this building. Inside, beyond a foyer in which there is a water basin for washing one's hands, a hall opens up which is not so large and from whose low ceiling there hang brass lamps, in a simple form, bulbous or spherical; the hall is brightened or darkened by the time of day, like a painting, and yet is not allowed to be adorned with paintings themselves. In the center, raised by stairs, is the square-shaped enclosure in which the Torah is recited—the Torah, which is kept on the Eastern wall in an often reverently carved shrine and is draped with embroidery on silk or velvet, is written by a worshipful hand on parchment and rolled like the books of four thousand years ago, and here it is ceremonially unveiled. Here the single upholder of the

Jewish soul reveals itself: prayer. The kind of worship that has now also slowly evolved in the big cities of the East, presumably in accordance with the West and non-Jewish rituals—the kind of worship service in which the prayer leader is the main axis around which the congregation orients itself like a rusty wheel, passive to the point of silence during the singing of the song leader and even of the chorus—is not to be found here. Here the prayer leader is nothing other than a loud voice among many, the designated keeper of the rhythm which moves all worshipers, each in and of himself. The commonality of this congregation stems more from the mutually governing soul of all its members than from the uniformity of the scripture. Connected to all others, each praying Jew is the sole representative of the communal prayer, his voice carried forth from all others to God, to whom all open themselves in this prayer, and his body, representative of devotion, sways back and forth, forward and backward, the deeper he absorbs himself in prayer, the higher his state of rapture. The prayer shawl in the "liberal" West is often merely a prim and superfluous ritual item, coyly folded into a stole and glimmering with its golden- or silver-woven trimming. In the East, it swathes the worshiper, it liberates the contour of his shape, separates him from the world, and often, wrapped over his head as well, it extinguishes the light of this world so that the divine light may shine all the more brightly.

Yes, prayer is still loud in the East. In each hour of praying, bit by bit, the embers of a charge toward the height of the Lord are kindled. And to superficial Western eyes and ears, this leaves an embarrassing and tasteless impression: these relentless voices, these jolting figures, these foreign articulated, wailing, groaning melodies, which storm together in a wild, screaming chorus and resonate like the rush of a distant surge, like the shouting of a wild mass, even outside the building's walls. Yet anyone who has been able to observe an Islamic mosque during prayer would recognize the Oriental in the Jew. The rhythm that moves the body there is more despiritualized, less personal, more structured by order; it has left its mark on the more objective part of prayer. With the Jew, it remains more subjective, more formed by the drive of prayer and the individual soul of the worshiper according to the force of the hour. But this, too, exists in the Orient: put briefly, the praying Eastern Jew in his most extreme rapture is more closely related to the dervish than to any kind of modern Jew. That form of prayer—the self-absorption, the opening of oneself silently, in the Western gesture, to receiving heavenly peace— is exactly the opposite of the praying Eastern Jew's essence, which is motorized, dynamically driven, like an arrow shot from a bow.

Yet not even in this environment is it made entirely clear how much the Jew and the space in which he prays really belong to each other. Only in the small Beth Ha-Midrash, the so-called *Bessmedresch*—which is no larger than an oversized study and of which there are many in every city, hidden in alleyways, high up in houses, or behind several courtyards— only in them is it revealed. In this study are a large heater, a small shrine for the Sefer Torah, several benches, which also fill the main prayer hall, desks with candleholders, and, here more remarkable than elsewhere, walls covered with thick tomes. During the four hours of prayer—early in the morning, before noon, in the afternoon, and around sundown— the *Bessmedresch* is filled with worshipers, and here they are purer and more liberated than in a large space. Here the prayer leader is the person to whom the honor was expressly granted, and there is no greater honor to be given.

But also at all other hours of the day and night there are Jews huddled together among themselves. Their profiles and their hunched shoulders stand out animatedly and touchingly from the geometric ornaments on the wall of books. Here they sit, having come in from the street, weary, reclining, tattered, and ordinary. And while seated, a bit of tranquility reaches them, relaxation, relief. It is winter, and so they seek the pleasing warmth of the heater and their relaxing eases into sleep. The sleeping Jew disturbs nobody, and nobody disturbs him. He is at home: this is everybody's house and thus also his house. Next to him, some talk about the daily events in the city or about the general spirit of the times—times that agitate the Jew all the more deeply the more defenselessly he gets caught up in them. Others discuss a business deal, while somebody reads

the newspaper. In a corner a latecomer is praying his solitary prayer; his prayer shawl is his shield. And just after he has finished, he immediately cuts into the conversation of one of the groups, or he acts like the sleeper. For in the East there is not the division that has made life in the West so full of order, stiffness, and empty disguise: here the place of prayer and nothing else, there the place of politics, of business, of rest. Instead of such division, here the one flows into the other, one carries the other and endures it. The souls suddenly gather together for the one activity and suddenly throw themselves into the next. The devotion does not allow for any disturbance, the ecstasy knows no interruption. And God, who is the creator and father of humankind, appears to the Jew not as a limiting and captivating being who allows for no violation of his space, but rather as a being so supreme and at the same time so basic, so gracious, and so familiar, that in his presence every ordinary social level of the Jew, of his beloved and his official possession, appears welcome and free. At least this is how the Jew experiences it. He is at home where his Lord is, and this space, the house of prayer and house of teaching, is just as much a house of the people as a house of God. That is why meetings can be held there—mundane meetings that deal with the problems and needs of the community—without the thought ever coming to anybody that this might be sacrilege; least of all the observant Jew should think this, for he knows that the bridge to God does not take root on any given premises, but in the souls of those praying.

Is this Jew praying? One could swear he is. Between his face and the book in his hand there is an unrestrained magnetic connection. The old and heavy lines of his face, carved out by life, are now channels for a kind of attentiveness which is the astonishing glorification of the spirit. His mouth, opened as in prayer, speaks silently the words that resonate in his heart. His hand, which holds the book, is placed like a mirror under his face, as if reflected in the white water of his beard were his concentrated spirituality; and like a little animal, expressive, adept, and composed, the other hand, still vulnerable and shy, ventures out of the hole, the cuff, in his ragged, broad sleeve. However, this person with the appearance of

rapt contemplation is not praying, he's reading. And the Jew with the book: that is indeed the true Jew. Here spread out before him are landscapes on the level of his original home, reaching infinitely to the horizon of the unknowable. Here he knows all dangers and overcomes all; and here, too, the frequently persecuted and scarce survivor of life finally feels free, productive, and powerful. Here he plays like an athlete with his powers. It is no doubt true that in this joy and security there also lies a hidden danger: the denigration of life. But this only threatens the young, for the old man, tired from the harassment endured from this merciless and evenly matched adversary, may rightfully seek refuge here. Thus, that is what he does.

The book is everything to him, for in glorious myths, the creation of words out of the fire of the divine throne is placed at the beginning of all creation. For him, the world regulates itself in the book: that which has been adopted from it in books, that alone is worthwhile and important; all other manifestations come second to books. And that is why he is so grateful and happy when his native environment and people like him are brought into being in books and are considered worthy of representation. Only then are this environment and the Jew himself given the dignity and permanence of truly vital things. This feeling is perhaps one of the reasons that the Jewish epic has achieved such success; and even if in the Hebrew language, in the holy tongue, a writer molds such subjects into his work, he will be eternally praised as deeply as the modesty of the Jew is otherwise able to keep such feelings from himself. Because of this attitude, the Hebrew poet and the Yiddish poet alike are shown splendor and love that only simple people are capable of giving to their artists. Bialik's or Schneur's prestige among Eastern Jewry is incomparable to that of the more abstract, less consistent, ineffectively admired, or quite simply famous German poets of the same order. And only the distinct adoration that Stefan George has inspired within his circle is to be compared with this type of natural and fervent prestige and leadership. Here, however, it is the poor and the ordinary, not the extremely erudite with the highest education, who love their poets: Mendele and Sholem

Aleichem, Asch and Agnon, and, above all, the magnificent Yitzhak Leyb Peretz. They are sons of the people, and an entire people is their enthusiastic, grateful, passionate readership. The Jew who holds a book in his hand, that is the armed and consoled Jew; he lives in landscapes which are devoid of sorrow and sin.

Yet, what is there to say about the Jew who, either at the Beth Ha-Midrash or at home, pores over a tractate from the Talmud spread out before him? The ring is closed around him, and he is happy. There is a tender smile on his lips, and in the deep shadow of his gaze is the rapt contemplation of total serenity. The portion of the book that lies before him represents a reflection and demystification of the world, a guide through all the confusions of life, and at the same time, in its complexity, it is a spiritual effort, a task and exercise of the highest order. It is also, for him, an act of religious worship, the fulfillment of one of the main commandments. To search among the teachings, that means to learn Talmud. He says "learning" per se, for it is in essence an infinite task, and only through unremitting, lifelong, total immersion is one able to approach it. The pure understanding of the problem at hand is to the foreigner an unfamiliar difficulty. For the Talmud is first of all a protocol, a record of the discussions (Gemara) in the houses of learning in Babylon (and Jerusalem). What is discussed is the use of the orally transmitted and later transcribed teachings (Mishnah) in the lives of the Jews during that time—under the circumstances in those lands around the year 200 to 400, according to our calendar—in the Syrian Aramaic language which the Jews then used. Each decree in the Mishnah is connected to a passage from the Torah, the Hebrew-language Pentateuch. The justification of a decree does not occur in a logical-causal fashion, but rather either mnemotechnically, that is, according to a word—and here the manifold meanings of one and the same Hebrew word are used generously— or according to analogies of other words from the Torah which have an inner connection to the passage at hand. The interpretation of such words is then discussed according to the different traditions that are practiced, and indeed often between the adherents of two different schools, one stricter and the other more liberal. They discuss not only the facts or the meanings, but above all the principles of thought according to which decisions are made. This is always done with regard to a particular case which ultimately loses its uniqueness and takes on exemplary importance. And that is why every now and then people who know nothing about all this and who merely perceive the bare word hear in this most profound, astonishingly sagacious book an absurd, wild, almost nonsensical kind of hair-splitting; they only hear their own ignorance.

Even the champions of dialectical training in the Gemara confuse a side effect with the main task: to inscribe in the law the entire life of the Jew (of the human being) and all his customs, all the many twists and surprises of the day and the hour, in such a way that the verdict and the life of the wisest and purest teachers become definitive for every Jew, yet not in such a way that finished tracts, which spare him the burden of decision, are handed over to him. Rather, it is done in such a way that spirit and awareness of the essential are awakened in him, and thus his thought becomes capable of drawing from the particular case the principle of its coming into being, then once more sinks back into the round fullness of the present moment, and then, his eyes fixed upon the event and at the same time surveying it from above, grants the particular case full justice. This is why the Talmud, which itself is made up of commentary and which has been continuously interpreted from Rashi and the Tosafists onward, is today a literature of twenty thousand volumes, a radically abstract and just as radically world-oriented intellectual tradition, method and meaning, thought process and deliberation, history and unavoidable presence. It is the mind of the Jew. It is the Jewish people once over. It is the assertion of God in human life. And it is full of wisdom and full of examples. For in the lessons and proverbs of the teachers and disciples there is always a human being involved, a pure and full character. The essences of entire human lives, achieved or pursued in inner unity, are often expressed in one sentence. They are told with the traits of the lives of the masters and the disciples, who themselves are also teachers and in whom characters can be recognized whose humility and purity affects and shocks those of us who are ambivalent and unspiritual. Yes, it is wisdom above all that is in the Talmud, not cleverness or knowledge or philosophy or theology, but the wisdom of life itself. To grow up in this atmosphere and to be educated by way of these examples and the surrounding ideas of human possibility, that gives young Talmud students, and old ones too, an aura of the purity of knowledge-for-the-sake-of-life about which we proud Occidentals learn to be silent. The fact that after the mastery of such complex study the Eastern Jew finds our science and philosophy easy should be noted merely as an aside.

And thus one sees in the evening and at night in the *Bessmedresch* or at home these old men with their large, rough workman's hands, their faces contorted or altogether vacant, after an entire day of earning their bread, sitting in front of a tractate from Gemara, seldom alone, often in pairs, "studying"—as if one were to see one's old cobbler or coachman at the day's end immersed in Kant's critiques or Marx's *Capital*. Quietly mumbling, quietly singing, they read the text aloud and bring it close to themselves by rendering it into Yiddish, comparing and applying commentator after commentator, all of this in an entirely unmelodic melody. For the fact that this spiritual activity is not performed silently or in spoken terms but uttered with inflections of singing and humming gives it the impression and enrapturing quality of great lyrical poems or incantations. The melody replaces the verse.

The man's upper body must join the melody, reaching a swinging motion which expresses the full subjugation of the motorized Jew to the spiritual mood. In this swaying of his body all of the diffuse special forces and intentions of the entire being are caught and diverted; they are rendered innocuous by the Jew, as by the Indian, through the absolute lack of movement. And when two studying Jews sit together, humming and swaying in front of the volumes with their hard-to-read print, whose Aramaic or Hebrew type, always in different styles and without vowels, represents Mishnah, Gemara, and commentary, pausing and always deriving from a passionate speech of which one understands as little as from the argument between two mathematicians—right at the difficult spot in

a long, complex formula, they turn intermittently toward the problem, in thesis and antithesis, discovering the difficulties in turning here and there, always allowing for new facets of contradictions to flash through their minds, until the principle of agreement between all modes of all times suddenly reveals its great triumph, which is secured a priori by way of the origin of all human knowledge from the single divine wisdom, until the proper standpoint is found from which one can observe the synthesis. When two inconspicuous Jews study together, they have both behind them and among them an intellectuality, an intellectual ancestral lineage and apogee of being in the face of which every other Middle Eastern tradition *[Volkstum]*, in terms of intellectual capacity, sinks into the paleness of primitive beginnings. Here lies the root of an intellectual power which forces the Jew to reach the top everywhere that thinking and the ability to think are required. It should be said that from such ability and training, tradition and requirement (for boys between the ages of twelve and fifteen need to be capable of reconstructing from memory the most complex problems and thought processes, so far as they have "learned" them, in an examination) an unpleasant development can also arise, namely, that a purely dialectical gambling frenzy may be substituted for knowledge, moral equivocation and self-deception for ethical strengthening. However, there is no natural or spiritual power which does not also carry with it dangers, and "where there is danger, there also grow the redeeming forces."

And so the Jew roots himself in the abstract, he draws rich currents of life out of this and turns them upward into the working sphere. Yet how does he set forth in the concrete, in his existence, in this wealth of color, wealth of desire, growing wealth of contours in his existence? This Jew, with his ceremonial fur cap upon his head and wrapped entirely in his prayer shawl, directs a composed and tender gaze toward the object in his hand: he is celebrating a holiday, a summer or harvest holiday, the Feast of the Tabernacle [Sukkoth], and the object in his hand is a bundled bouquet of willow, myrtle, and palm leaves, a ceremonial bouquet whose necessary supplement is a lemon-like fruit, the "Essrig," a fragrant

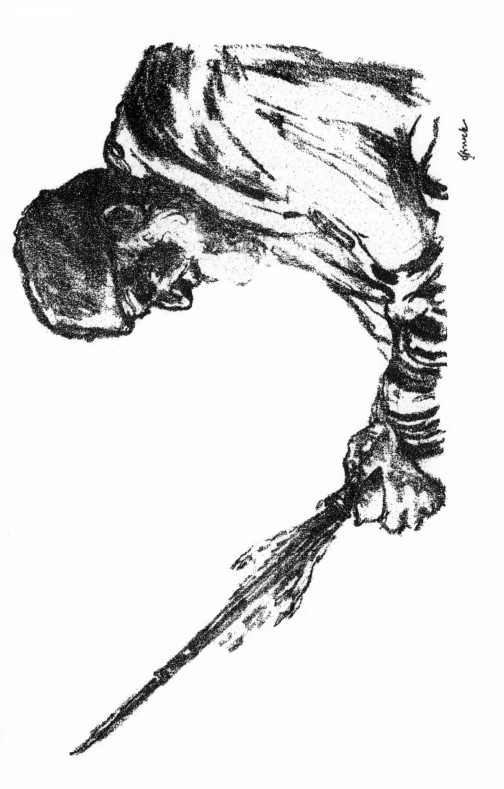

fruit from Palestine. However, from all that this fruit and bouquet mean in real life, from the laughing and the happiness, the shining and the sumptuously decorative, there is nothing left other than an object of ritualistic care and anxieties, an object which at certain moments in the act of prayer is shaken, carried around, and used together with blessings. Nothing of the high celebratory and vital feeling flutters around this bouquet any longer—there is nothing bouquet-like about it—and as a result, it becomes a fully real symbol. For the Eastern Jew, the concrete links to the high, celebratory life are weakened to the point that the ceremony is no longer understood in its true sense—no more elevated, rejoicing, grateful, vital feeling that works according to the rhythm of the year. That is the price that the Jew has had to pay.

In the West, the ceremonial gatherings of ancient Israel have become occasions for a modified order of prayer, for a break from work, better meals, and a walk perhaps. But they are no longer celebrations. One may care to ask the bitter question: where in Europe are there real celebrations? Here, too, the Jew has gone to the extreme; yet the malady is a general decline, and we do not want to take special account of the contribution that he has made to it. Rather, it is merely the fact that one who lives in the extreme, with an exuberance of the soul that pours forth so strongly into prayer, has found no connection to the vital feeling of celebrations; he finds no appeal in them, he does not feel affected. It has become self-evident that it is this way for him. Where does the European Jew have direct access to the passing of the year? This urban dweller in his little street? And how should celebrations ensue from concrete events when the events themselves, though they once produced such celebrations, now lie in the prehistory of the people and have become mere abstractions? The liberation from Egypt, the creation of the commandments at Sinai, the rescue from the eternal enemy Haman's hands, the reconstruction of the Temple: he feels them and their substance. Their respective meanings are conveyed to him. Only the commitment to the celebratory, only the sympathy with it has faded. The original high spirits of the Purim celebration, its costumes and games, are barely—indeed, only weakly—still enlivened.

And yet in the Eastern Jew the fullest capacity for celebration, for celebratory jubilation, is still there. For the eight days of this Feast of the Tabernacle is a true celebration—but this jubilation pours forth from the joy in the Torah, in its teachings, whose last passage is read aloud as part of the ceremony, establishing the cycle of the year. On this day the Torah rolls are taken from the ark, which otherwise serves as shelter, and with the Torah, his holy beloved, the Jew dances in the house of its teachings; he dances a seemingly endless, wild dance. He dances around before God, animated by the powerful and monotonous melodies. The Torah rolls are passed from arm to arm, and dust and stomping fill the room, which sees such an event only once a year. Not outdoors in the grass, not in the intoxicating and exalted light does the Jew dance for his God this David-like dance—but he dances. And it is only in this dance that one profoundly feels one's alienation from all that is natural, from all that keeps the Eastern Jew preserved. These old men, more the men than the boys, who really romp and rejoice in the prayer halls, these jumping Jews with blowing *Tallejssim* [prayer shawls] and quivering beards, dance naturally without women, dance as the Orientals they are in honor of the festive celebration and according to the book that contains the path to God, the path to life. These dancers evoke the quivering in and of itself, and with this the one real insight is received: how far one is alienated from life itself. Even the children, with their blue and white banners and small flags, with their raisins and other modest delicacies, are led down the same path: Simchat Torah, "Ssimchestoire," is the only Jewish children's celebration in the East . . .

If the Eastern Jew should no longer understand the joy that pours forth from life, the sorrow is conveyed to him all the more deeply, the sorrow that pours forth from the fate of the Jewish Nation, from the Jewish people. Yes, here he is: Job among the peoples, ahead of all others, leading them, unreachable by them. The ninth day of Ab, this same day that twice witnessed the destruction of the Temple, the destruction of the people, is a true and passionate point of despair in all Jewish congregations. In slippers and soft shoes—taking off one's boots is the first sign of the Oriental in mourning—they enter the houses of learning; they huddle on the floor or sit on low benches and stools, small candles next to them, a small book in their hands. In semi-darkness, their faces become pale silhouettes. And between two candles the prayer leader begins to read the lamentations of Jeremiah, to sing, in a cutting and sobbing melody, monotone and disquieting in the constant return of its long, modulated, lamenting tones. And that is the representation of the insecurity of life itself, which here is increasingly brought to a state of trembling. The dead not just from that year, but from many besiege the souls of the Jews who refrain from meals for twenty-four hours. The dead from the Middle Ages return, the dead from the endless Middle Ages that envelop the Jews: the abundance of beatings from all the days of persecution and pogroms return, all houses of prayer are crammed with souls that drift around the candles. The horror at the rawness of one's fellow human being, who in every furious and hateful disturbance attacks the defenseless with physical devotion to the law of least resistance, leads to a terrible feeling of being transitory among the living. And here, around the defenseless Jew, the glory of the constantly persecuted is aroused.

On the ninth day of Ab, in the middle of the glare of the European summer, the Jew links himself to a chain which binds him to all of his dead ancestors; he visits the cemeteries and sees the stones that announce past visitors. Mourning and despair stand in place of the joy and pleasure of the harvest; here the Jew lives intensely with the reality of destruction, in a way that no Western people is capable of. The feeling of being threatened nationally, which pulsates only weakly in those defeated and lamed in the world war, such that there was not even a trace of true public mourning, this feeling floods the Jew more genuinely than is imaginable to the foreigner. For the Jew, the act of mourning, everlasting over centuries and entirely one with the terrible present, is also a productive act: it is aimed at his own being and essence; and when he calls out for redemption and, in hatred, against the sinner and murderer, indeed he

beats first and foremost against his own breast; he has betrayed his goal and his path, he has sinned against the spirit, he himself belongs to the original source of grief and shame, not the others, the foreigners, the enemies! How could they beat and kill him, the Jew, the servant of God, if he hadn't so miserably distanced himself from his sources and the essence offered to him! This inward turn, symbol of national virtue, of Jewish obligation and of human maturity, is at the same time the source of renewal and eternal regeneration: this turn, so it appears, is not understood by the European, at least not the German, who looks obsessively for foreign causes of his unrest and who merely stews in his hatred, regardless of whether it is aimed at the Englishman, the Frenchman, or the Jew . . . The physical law of least resistance is acutely awakened in him, even today. Poor conquered soul without the fruit of defeat . . .

The Jew carries his past with him, hunched over but untiring. He tilts his strong shoulders, servant of God that he is, and with his knees bent he slowly walks toward the destination that is determined for him in order to carry the past into the future. For it is not an empty load, not abandoned iron from a conquest, not a fruitless stone; it is the nourishing fruit of his spiritual earth. In the twilight, he will lower it down and he himself will lie down to die, for he wishes to rest. But just as he has inherited it from his father, so, too, shall his son carry it further. Tradition is the word that his load and his nourishment express. With incomparable power, he brings to life that which in other cultures would long have been considered dead weight. For him, as for all people without land and borders, it is a matter of guaranteeing the continuation of that which is holy, and again to push forward toward unlimited life on earth; this is indeed for him a self-evident value, but above all it is the vehicle of divine fulfillment. For him, the present and the near past—near, to be sure, for a people with a consciousness that extends six thousand years—are like the terrible fulfillment of prophetic curses.

Aberrations have taken hold—fatigue of religious observance, loss of self, desire and yearning for the easy life of others—and with them the horrible fulfillment of the curse and revenge, hate, blood and death,

contempt and shame, persecution across the entire earth: all words of the prophets, their worst dreams and most excessive curses. And from them the Jew derives boundless faith that the soft, gentle, blessed part of these expressions should also be fulfilled—all that is terrible in the present, with the power to console, guarantees the glory that follows. And since he is a Jew, he knows how deep the level of human interaction is in his fate, namely, that the ruling Lord has deemed him worthy of being involved in the work of redemption and nothing from above shall be cast down. Rather, the riches of well-being lie in the courage and action of the human being; he learns the task of helping to prepare for that which shall come one day, in that he persists, does not die out, does not dry up. Here there is no border between the national and the religious for him, rather only the unity of the people as representatives and supporters of divine grace. Thus, not a single scrap of tradition may be abandoned, for then there is no more enduring. Every spiritual precaution is allowed, where it serves to support the very building, the Chinese wall, around the Jewish people; even the lowest commandments, whose observance may perhaps appear senseless, are brought to life and made indispensable by a greater purpose. One begs for the falling of dew and rain, without owning an acre of land, during times when dew and rain are necessities in Canaan; one retains the age of sexual maturity among boys, even though in the European milieu, there is no physical demand for that. One is wary of recognizing in religion a woman's independent position, which has long been a fact of daily life. And since children are the guarantors of survival, even in times of misery, which are made still worse by additional births, a large number of children is a blessing. Thus tradition—law and the teachings, the center of life and passionate resistance—becomes aware of the deep distrust with which every movement seeking to loosen the spell of the law has to grapple. For tradition considers itself certain of the continuation of the Jewish people and, above all, of the key to the eternal Jewish task: to establish, on another basis, the sanctification of life.

There have always existed such social movements, because life, the sustaining power of the people itself, has thrown itself against the wall of tradition from time to time. It must indeed appear impossible that a people, even with a resilient past, with so inexhaustible a richness of life and such vigorous existential joy, could ever overcome such a blow. The power of the essence and its vitality itself are bestowed upon all of these attempts at liberation: effectiveness and fullness, resonance and character. From this same power Jewish nationalism and the Socialist movement, the Enlightenment *(Haskalah)* and Hasidism derived their allure. The first three of these movements, founded in the West, only infringed mildly upon the Eastern Jewish people; but the fourth, indeed incomparable, movement burst directly out of them: Hasidism. Today in the West one knows about it mainly from the writings of Martin Buber, which are only introductions and which—nobody knows this better than Buber himself—are provisional in their explanations and have not yet received adequate expression in their development. Still, the outlines of the Baal Shem, of this stunning and totally pure human being, and of his great-grandson, Rabbi Nachmann of Bratslav, which are contained in both books that our teacher has given us, remain pure and shining. We also thank Buber, to whom we owe so much, for the interpretation of this religious phenomenon which still today has a presence within Eastern Jewry, even if it is not quite the same as that which once poured forth from the Baal Shem and his real disciples.

The original source of Judaism, its vital unwritten devotion to action, has been brought to light once again. Not learning but active inner life, not the book but the human being, community, and nature have become the primacy of Jewish existence. And so we encounter today—though only in the remote regions to which the destiny of war has brought us— such Jews, who appear given to the purity, serenity, and simplicity with which the teachings of Hasidism have acted against the teachings of violence. This encounter restores the shimmer of divine presence to the simple, pure human being of ordinary life, of daily life. He who lovingly and happily faces his fellow human beings with self-abandon and inner humility, not isolated but feeling part of the community, who approaches his workday in pure spirit and with pure hands, is no lower than the person who studies day and night. This simple, uneducated Jew, who sits with his entirely modest soul, unconcerned with profit, weaving stockings or restoring clocks: he too is righteous, he too serves God. And through this turn, the life of the simple workers is at once redeemed and consecrated; the inexpressible serenity of the good conscience is again present; yes, joy comes to them and transforms these poor, burdened peopled into a warm humanity and dignity. It intones in the often wordless dances and melodies of the Hasidim with an enchanting rhythm; even today, it expresses its movements and relaxed gestures. For all of this, they still have their helper and advocate, who advises them consolingly in the difficult dilemmas of life: the zaddik, the chosen and sanctified one whose prayers have a magical effect and who feels the will of God and may even apply it . . .

These teachings bring enormous relief to the hard life of the poor Jew and also give an ultimate reflection of the great nature surrounding him. As long as the Baal Shem and his disciples have rediscovered the delight of earth and placed it in its divine virtue, something such as this may well be eclipsed, but it will not get lost. For these small Eastern cities, embedded in nature, have to be conscious, always and ever anew, of the brightness of the field in the first green and of the liberating air that blows out of the forests. Out of the mystical teachings of Hasidism there came very little obscure negation of earth; the battle of the human soul remained directed at the earthly deed, and even the transmigration of the soul, which it absorbed and developed, brought about earthly affirmation. Even if the goal was to live in such a way that one would not need to start from scratch a new evolutionary path, but rather could enter the redeemed community of the pure, our existence remained on earth, and the fulfillment of our tasks remained the only path toward realizing this goal. And that is why it was possible to be brought not into a state of frantic, gloomy, negative repentance—for nobody knows the reason for one's rebirth—but toward full devotion to performing pure, human-loving, and inspirational pious activities. Only one who knows the

magnitude of the contribution to working professions among the Jews can measure how much this says in favor of Eastern Jewry. In fact, one would not attach so much value to stupid speeches about the mercantile nature of Eastern Jews if one were to cite the figures about the distribution of professions that were given to us in the most recent Russian census. According to the census, craftsmen, manual workers, and the like made up more than 53 percent of all employed Jews, dealers and merchants only 31 percent—this, however, in the entirely abnormal conditions of the saturated Western Zone, filled with Jews and once part of the former empire. Even more telling are the figures in places where the Jew chooses more freely what he does: for example, in turn-of-the-century New York, where of the Eastern Jewish immigrants, 61.08 percent of men and 71.80 percent of women were employed in the areas of crafts and production, in comparison to 38.04 percent of men and 36.07 percent of women from the total population. One can only pity the person who, based on the manifold sick conditions of the German occupation, pontificates about the Jew's desire or lack of desire to work.

Let us rather return to our chief domain: the Jew of the East is ready for work, in handicrafts above all, because in order for him to feel like a living person, he must have a place—and not in an impersonal factory—in which his occupation can be fulfilled. This cobbler who hammers soles in a tiny workshop, entirely immersed and lost in the fortune of being able to work, that is the true Jew of the East. For a productive person nearly has to be physically violated not to want be active with the entire body, with eyes and muscles; and life among the primitive people *[im niederen Volk]* is not yet degenerate; the atrophy of joy in using one's body is part of the existence of the merchant (and the student). Work is in every sense an antidote to worries; the Eastern Jew's belief in God's aid never leads to the rejection of work, but rather labor and its fruits are the representatives of divine assistance. And only he who can no longer work, and must beg, is truly abandoned and poor . . . It hardly bears mentioning that the work of the Jew is honest and faithful service. To have learned what one does and to perform what one has learned as well as possible:

this craftsman's attitude, which needs merely to be raised to a higher sphere in order to approach the spirit of the true creator, of the artist, this attitude is alive in the Eastern Jew as in every craftsman. It, too, is religiously grounded and consecrated. Whoever squanders his time on the fruitless, superficial hustle and bustle squanders his life and wastes that which was given to him in the service of God; he is without solidarity, as the swindler has no community *[Gemeinschaft]*. Therefore, one is much more likely to have something to complain about in the tardiness of the Eastern Jewish craftsman—as with every craftsman—than in bad work. Because one likes to promise a rush, which is always important to the customer and which one would like to perform if only the work to be carried out didn't always need more time than one imagined . . . There's often a charming sense of humor among these old-fashioned men, who remain a good ways behind the European times. In many cities of the East, especially in the big ones, the Pole has surpassed them, and as a small-time industrialist, he has incorporated the modern pace and the machine into his work more easily than the Jew, for whom the different conception of time—work without spirit, without spiritual involvement, and instead only with intellectual involvement—has penetrated his lifestyle so much more slowly. Here work and soul are still unified—to bring to life an attitudinal element to which one feels connected whether one works or broods, prays or worries, that is the guarantor of radiant beauty. And as split as the soul of the Jew may appear to be, in its duality between the misery of the present and the joy of the future, here it is not divided, but instead a vestige of richness and unity that transforms the worker into a human being, a human being created by God.

But the Jew, too, must sustain the general curse of the times, and he has become ugly. Just as often as the beauty of the noble spirit may wish to show its face with the brightness of a deep and high forehead, the Jew's daily life is spoiled by gloominess and lack of color, filth and poverty. Here you see him stretched across the front of his cart, with his shoulders pressed into the straps like a horse pulling a buggy, his fists clenching the

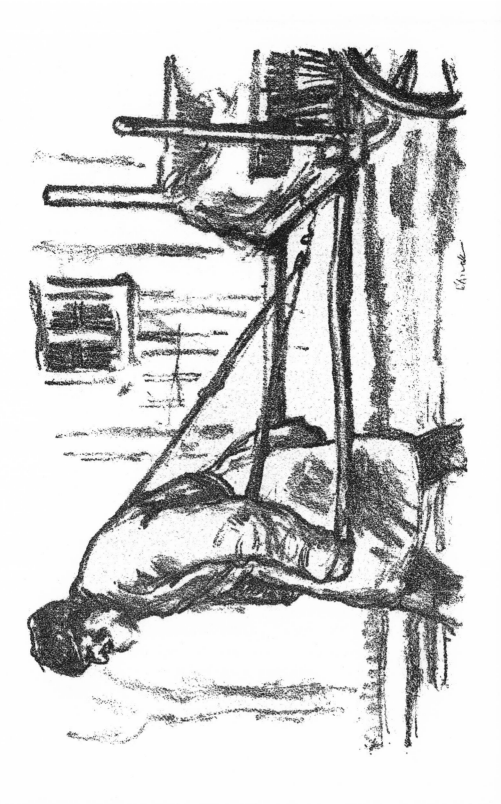

handles as if they were part of his harness. An animal in its yoke, as poor and downtrodden as it may be, is more beautiful than he; indeed, even a sled dog, the abused racing dog from the prairie, or the captured hunting dog has more grace than he. The beauty of the human being, the liberating and divine light become imperceptible in him, buried beneath a thick ash. In the daily life of the Eastern Jew it is no longer a viable force, this beauty which for the ancient Jew was as strong as the biblical hymns suggest. Only the young girls and the children still have it, but that is not relevant here. For the Eastern Jew, the beauty of life—namely, as a yearning, as a goal—is greeted with suspicion; he turns his back on it, timidly or enraged. It is foreign, it is the mask of the "evil force," it is the enemy. It is sensuality and freedom. It defies the law, it lures the human being toward foreign modes of living, it is a threat to continuity. To acquire such a precious commodity as continuity, one must make large sacrifices, and this side of one's existence, the lightest, must be sacrificed. It is indeed the source from which all of life's temptations come, it seduces the young. To see in the epitome of evil an erotic sensuality and to toss the beauty of life into the radical renunciation of it: that is the terrible perception that modern Judaism has brought into the world—it is the flip side of a spirituality which was taken up by Nordic tribes, but which has been discovered to pose an extraordinary threat to the people of the Mediterranean.

For the Jew, the "Epicurean," the "Apikoyres" is the damned itself. Of course, this struggle and the nonsense directed at such a life-affirming and glorious phenomenon shows how strong this propensity still is in the Jew; only in him, the good conscience, courage, joy, affirmation has changed fully and radically into the opposite. As soon as this demon appears, the Jew loses his bearing and his mind; the way he is today, he feels like a spade has cut into his roots. Freedom of life, beauty of life: that marks the abandonment of the discipline of God. Whoever wishes to live happily—happy in the sense of the original free human being—is cursed; whoever wishes to express one's personality playfully and plainly, also in the sensual sphere of life, ceases to wish to approach God. One can sanctify life with all desires, just not sensuality and beauty. (The Baal Shem thought otherwise.) And thus the Eastern Jew of the older generation knows only one freedom: that of sacrifice. To make a concession in this area is unthinkable to him. For him, the sensual has become impure insofar as it is not directed toward marriage and the will to procreate; he rejects with such great vehemence all demands of the modern sensibility—those that allow the true human community to be thought of as marriage, one which will have died without the seduction of a sensuality satisfied within itself according to the will of affection—that understanding is not possible. "Beauty," when applied to the Jew—"a beautiful Jew"—means that the Jew is of a religiously observant, charitable, pure nature, devoted to the Torah and learning and prepared for the will of God. Beauty is allowed only in reference to the soul. Yet the body of the human being is his seduction, his temptation, his malady. The body does not exist in the true sense. It is an animal on which the soul of God rides, it is a stubborn mule, one that is whipped and kept in a state of hunger.

There is an endless array of perspectives concerning this phenomenon, and it does not appear possible to attend to them all. One can say, sociologically speaking, that this ugliness is typical of the petit bourgeois: everything thus deducible to the Eastern Jew as a people of the lower middle class. Or one can refer to the physical ugliness of the Jew as a Dorian Gray phenomenon: thus, the ugliness of the soul is personified by its oppressor, its tormentor, its persecutor. Every ugly and coyly corrupting Jew conveys to the hunter Edom: I am you, look at your ugly and distorted soul spread out upon me. And yet here, in not so much explaining as describing, expounding upon what is vital, we do not dare think of pursuing an apology for the Jew. Rather, we must speak of the extension of this beauty antagonism, of the positive half of the antinatural judgment, but only briefly, since it is all too indisputable: the Eastern Jew has subdued his sexuality and on the level of this strong, bursting sexual instinct, he has built a foundation of morality. "Not as you like, but rather as I like," he tells his instinct. And if one could see these men, the broad, heavy, powerful coachmen, pack carriers, blacksmiths! How these black-bearded fellows keep struggling with the demon that is as strong as they are. This bull-necked and by no means intellectualized group of people with its awakened and craving desires! Then one could compare, the West could compare, as it so often does, this Jewish man in a society of men with non-Jews of the same class. Thank God, it often comes down to amusing crudities, but it never comes down to the dirty joke, to the mindless, stinky joke that characterizes the German urban and rural laborer (read: to a member of the armed forces). The Jew controls his sexuality; for him, a woman is never merely the personification of a sexual organ, as she is for others, but a human being. Here is a general purity of feeling which has nothing to do with repression. Indeed, we know today that every form of discipline and sublimating control of a desire, and especially of this desire, is mistaken for its opposite, for repression by the intellectual dilettantes—and, alas, how widespread this group is today.

But this is not the place to inquire further as to how much real repression undermines the structure of the Jew, and whether or not among the effects of the pleasure in beauty and of the thirst for reaching the superficial world—in appearance, in power, and in a liberated sense of one's body—repression of a dangerous kind is carried out. (Perhaps herein lies, as far as it is affirmed by individual Eastern Jews, the source of Bolshevist terror.) Only at the point at which a desire becomes strictly defined, where its existence is recognized and is taken into hand, can one no longer speak of repression, but of discipline and culture. Yes, here sexuality, this destructive and menacing demon of the bourgeois world, has been compelled without excuse to perform constructive work. This same demon, which otherwise would like to destroy continuity in the name of freedom, must in fact ensure continuity. It has been entirely routed into marriage—and there will still be much to say about that. As sure as it is that various enriching solutions to the problem of the affirmation and reclamation of emotions may appear, collectively, for an entire people, a comprehensive one has not yet been found. For the division of separate spheres of life, developed so splendidly by the ancient Greeks and so

grotesquely by the modern Europeans, has not yet been granted to the Jew who aims at unity.

Yet it is obvious that on this basis neither a societal culture nor a creative and receptive relation to fine art could be developed—with the single exception being the art that is effective in books or on the stage, in poetry and literature. The energy that flows directly from the spirit, the literary energy, could have a favorable effect. However, the spirit that communicates through various forms of masks and that baldly exhibits the sensuality of life, both as a creation and as a matter of taste, would necessarily have to waste away with the puritanical treatment of the sensual. In the aesthetic realm, the Eastern Jewish creative instinct became a guest of the West, albeit an insecure and embarrassed guest. Only very recently are there Eastern Jewish painters of the artistic caliber of Marc Chagall, and there are still few sculptors, architects, or even artisans commensurate with the long-established creative tradition of the writers; in this area there is no discerning taste among the public like that which exists in the literary realm. And as deeply enamored of cultural music the folk-song pioneering Eastern Jew may be, he has little interest in the grand musical tradition. He, who has so easily mastered abstract thought, barely understands the difference between the lyrical worldly spirit in German music and that of all other kinds; he rates it just as highly as the lyrical sensuality of the contemporary Italian variety, and on the next level, for him, is the sphere of the elegant-melancholic or the fiery-winsome music of an uninspired kind that the Poles or Russians have produced in the East. The worldly musical celebrations of the Eastern Jews do not have their own character—the exception once more being everything that has to do with weddings—and they distinguish themselves from other bourgeois functions only in the excess of performances, the inadequacy of the individual work, and the incongruity of the arrangement. The furniture in their homes is made up entirely of Western imports of the worst kind, their domestic appliances the same, and even if men's traditional dress expresses its own style through the long, old-fashioned German gown (one calls it a caftan in the West)—to which the festive

fur-brimmed *streymel* adds a dignified touch—women's dress is simply that of the Warsaw or Viennese West, the West in general, and worn sometimes with good, other times with bad affectations. Among individual Jewish women it produces much tact and sense not for beauty, but for chic style. Domestic behavior and manners are only expressed in an unconcerned and naive naturalness, which one receives without a particular "upbringing"—in showing warmth and fine feeling as well as tact on proper occasions.

Yet much to the dismay of the Western Jew—who for his part is not inclined to disregard "manners" and "tact," because he has just managed to beat them into his own head—the simple Eastern Jew is not "refined." Or so one thinks! He talks very loudly, doesn't know to keep his distance or show restraint, he chomps his food and slurps at the table, he puts his knife into his mouth . . . The Western Jew swoons with shame, for the non-Jew could somehow mistake him for an Eastern Jew, or could identify him as such! An oppressive narrowness encompasses all these areas of vital human consequence, and yet nothing tempts one as strongly toward flight from the Jewish environment as the sparkle, the brightness, and vastness that European life, despite all its misleading and falsifying qualities, extends to the Eastern Jew who becomes acquainted with it. Yet we ourselves know all too well that the charge derived from these conclusions has only little justification in being expressed aloud. For the Eastern Jew is in truth this human being who is bound to his machine, his back bent, pedaling and withering away, without air, light, or leisure, and must work to earn his paltry daily bread. The wheel hums, the dust flies up, his eyes bloodshot and tearing from fatigue, but in the overcrowded conditions of the "Tscherta" [precincts], as in the involuntary and voluntary ghettos of New York and London, only restlessness alone helps one earn his bread. The Eastern Jew knows that wherever there are Jews, no Jew shall die of hunger, and thus he goes to these new ghettos; he expects nothing but animosity from foreign people [*fremden Blute*]. And so there looms above an entire people the wretched and gloomy atmosphere of the unredeemable petite bourgeoisie, if not the horribly exploited and hopeless atmosphere of the proletariat. All working powers of this people are only capable of beating toward the inner core, of siphoning off their energy into the ethical sphere. The possibility of displaying, in one's external behavior or in the pleasant details of one's existence, joy in the world, the sweet life, brightened by divine freedom and human dignity, is cut off at the outset by lack of sustenance and, above all, lack of space. And in spite of this, directed by the merciless eye of an ambitious people, we have to give this cruelty our blessing. For if every inhibition toward the Eastern Jew were to be externally removed, if space in any arbitrary country in the great expanse of the Eastern and Western continent were to be made accessible to him: so great is the pressure of poverty, of affliction, and of desperate social forces that nothing guarantees that the Eastern Jew wouldn't reproduce explosively, spreading his seed like a piece of fruit that has burst, and the last closed ethnic enclave of the Jews would cast itself out as individuals. Hatred among people is a form of political self-fulfilling prophecy . . .

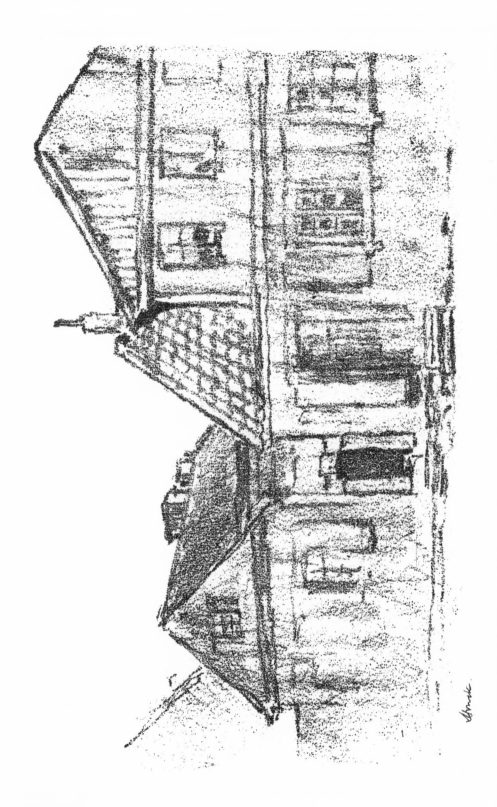

III.

These are the houses of the Jewish street: run-down, yellowed, decaying—
yet this is how they looked two generations ago, and it is unpredictable
how much longer they will stand on their own, if fire doesn't destroy them
first. They do not seem to have any particular form beyond that they are
deteriorated palaces or the former homes of old bourgeois families; atop
a formless facade, put up in a raw and unrefined fashion—owing to the
needs of cheap construction and lack of architectural feeling—and behind which an entire world can live—there sits an artless rectangular
gable. One of the doors to the building opens up to the street and behind it there is usually a dismal small shop, though often one enters the
building from the courtyard, in which a strip of grass is provided by nature's fidelity and even more often there are trees, friendly and breezy
trees. The shutters do not hang very geometrically, in terms of the an-
gles, and occasionally a piece of paper is stretched over a broken win-
dowpane, or they are hollowed out on all levels by generations of wear.
Only seldom do the chimneys reveal themselves as barren, forlorn cubes;
instead they sit like a physiognomy upon the roofs. Under them, however, built around the furnace, are rooms, true lived-in space filled with
people. They are poor, they make do without taste, but they are entirely
suffused with a hominess that rises above all else.

In each kind of people there seem to be two central links to their commonality: the one in which the creative, life-forming energies converge, and the other, which is part of the regenerative, life-continuing, and preserving forces. The one has long been a community *[Gemeinschaft]* of men—although the figures of Miriam, Moses' sister, and Deborah clearly demonstrate that for the Jew there was somehow a period in which it was made possible for women to play a central role in the active, official community. In Eastern Jewry, the Beth Ha-Midrash, the Beth Am, and the *Waad* are the sites in which male concerns, the official life of the Jewish community *[Gemeinde]*, and also the general political transactions of worldly life, the discussion and exchange of "didactic" and abstract questions (Gemara and its literature, cases of Talmudic law, and so on) characterize the atmosphere. The site of the other link is the home, its form the family.

"Family" and not "marriage" is the decisive word. For marriage is indeed for us the bond between man and woman, a closed relationship befitting of self-esteem in which the innermost conceivable form of community is experienced. Its values—unity, purity, richness of life, human evolution—are themselves realized in the alliance between two people. The tendency toward perpetuation inherent in marriage applies only to itself, not to some other community (e.g., nation, humankind); its indissolubility is merely the fruit of unified fundamental convictions. The production of offspring is a function of the Western marriage, but not its most essential; even without children, an authentic marriage is still consummated. This is not true for the family, and for the Eastern Jew, it comes down to that alone. For him, marriage is merely a prerequisite for family; after ten years, a childless marriage should in fact be terminated, since children are its necessary condition. Yet, children, who themselves provide the most important fulfillment of the law of humankind, testify that here the capability of self-perpetuation is allocated to the national concerns; family is the essence of the people in which it grows. For if children are also the prolongation of the individual into the future, and they transmit parental values, especially those that are vital and biological, then here the individual is himself primarily valued in terms of his vitality and is the bearer of his obligation to the people.

Family: with this word, an eternal and primal word of the human being is expressed, and nowhere does the deep and unshakable wisdom still alive in the Eastern Jew reveal itself more clearly. What the family is up against today—and presumably, it has never been more strongly attacked than these days, certainly not by Jews—sees only the squat, degenerate, crumbling final wall of this enormous foundation of human life. For today's family may be degenerate, that is rather certain. But its visual effect mistakes the passing decline for true destruction . . . There are lunar phases of eternal human phenomena: they decline, they lose their visibility and luminous intensity, they appear to fade. But in reality they are only the obscuring and vital rhythms of eternal being. Nietzsche pronounced God and religion dead and one believed him; and in the meantime, religious life is continuously growing among the best, its new form is a human-binding ethos, its allocated space is on earth, in the soul and the community. Art was similarly pronounced dead, and within it, new currents of energy are growing out of the religious. The eternal ideas—those that reveal themselves in the life of the community—fare no differently. The people *[Volkheit]*, long doomed to decline, rebuilds itself, determined to rid itself of the violence and of the violent state; humanity, entirely dismissive of nationalism in the nineteenth century, now grows increasingly fervent in its real nationalism; marriage and family, both of them corroding twenty years ago, are discredited today and they, too, are part of the same phenomenon. One merely has to have steady and farsighted vision to see these developments, and one may not attribute an overly humane concern to the present . . . We are all not as important as we think.

For if family were not just that, not an eternal phenomenon and one that is legitimate throughout eternity, who would bear this face *[Antlitz]*? This is the woman of the people, who sacrifices herself entirely for the good of the family, who offers herself to the family. Like the dark, startling face of a tortoise, the once glowing countenance peers out from her

large, shell-like scarf. The continuous burden of grief is the name of the demon that cursed the woman so horribly, unrelenting work the spell that turned her hands dry and hard like a skeleton. Affliction has carved the features of this decaying mouth; in the hard parchment of skin are her eyes, which can only see what is nearest: tomorrow's bread. She has given birth to children and raised them, and amid the misery of the times she has passed on that which she herself could not have co-created. But that is what her care, her motherly instinct, is there for: the eternally awakened heart in her breast has become the best nurturer and educator of the children. If her spirit is not enough to solve the various problems and clashes of youth, it is indeed all the more active in vigorously maintaining the physical and biological conditions that make it at all possible for the youth to exist. For the sorrows of youth, the harshness of the situation, and the battle against helplessness constitute formative elements of one's upbringing. It does not require much more if it is to become a human being with a promising future. Everyone grows up in life; the malleable and aggressive force of youth turns itself against its resistances all the more dramatically the lonelier that it is. Each upbringing is an occasion of loneliness, provided that the instincts of the young person remain intact. And of course there cannot be an all-too-perverse environment waiting for him. Even so, a strong youth can surmount such obstacles; but one has to foster those who are less strong, and this is indeed the place for the wise and passionate pedagogue.

What the family enables first and foremost—in being a key force of transmission, and in carrying life's gains and riches into the future—is the preservation of the physical foundation. And now in fact it appears that selecting the most individualized spouse possible serves as the norm, as the best-known prototype. Highly developed individuals do not carry the burden of self-perpetuation alone. Experiences gained long ago, currently examined more closely in the studies of Dr. Wilhelm Fliess, appear to have anticipated that only a limited duration and time is given to the human being—conceived in overly individualized terms and preserved in the family. The more pronounced the individual is, the more social energy is used in educating a single human being, and the sooner the duration of the family exhausts itself. That is why the continuity of a people, this eternal succession of families, is best preserved where the most well-balanced type possible defines the hereditary line and the essence of the people; that is, where resilience, the strength of resistance, and an aggressive physical élan find secure footing.

Having talents of all kinds is dangerous for a people that lives under such abnormal conditions as do the Jewish people. For the talented people, impatient as they are, have an effect on the newest and, as ambitious as they are, on the most widespread of currents: and through both, they make contact with the dominant culture. They assimilate themselves, most frequently in those places where they develop in violent contradiction to their families, and where only under protest have they become aware of the demands placed on them by the people; that is, where their talent is still connected to the steadfast, resilient, loyal character of their people only insofar as they are steadfastly, resiliently, and loyally against their individual task, but are no longer capable of or rich enough to affirm the links of such an overarching kind as ethnic traditions. Such appears to be the impersonal way in which marriages are generally consummated among Eastern Jews—indeed, it is also very common in Judaism in general. The national sense of marriage entirely appropriate to an endangered national tradition: it is the physical foundation of the prototype and sets up a dam for the individual who decontaminates the waters. Moreover, within the chief representative sectors of Eastern Jewry, the selection of a spouse is very little oriented toward the individual, much more toward generic values. One notes the futility of comparison when one compares the average Jew, thanks to the merits of his higher spiritual and ethical culture, to the educated European bourgeoisie (only in the question of manners and tact does this false perspective prevail); since the petit bourgeois [*Kleinbürger*] represents the main sector of Eastern Jews, one must place the average Jew next to the European peasants and workers, and only then does one recognize that also in these sectors there is no talk of a very individualized and personalized selection of spouse;

that here, too, one selects according to general predominant values. And once again, like everywhere else, in this the tragedy of our situation becomes apparent: nationally, we have to guard against our best, against the representatives of high personal values. Precisely those who render the ways and the greatness of our people most legitimate, those who are the pride and honor of every normal people, become dangerous for us—indeed, they are all the more dangerous the more frequently they emerge and the more marginal and cultivated the sectors become from which they spring up.

What kind of gratitude does the Jewish woman of the people receive for her difficult and valiant life? What is she then able to contrive, so composed and quiet, with her hands folded, looking at us with her clear eyes, peering out from all her folds and wrinkles? What gives her mouth, in spite of everything, this calm, composed serenity? She fades so quickly, the Oriental woman; the poverty barely recedes as a result of her indefatigable toils, which must constantly be carried out again by her many children in a very cramped household and which, often enough, she extends still further by running a small shop. What supports her? The answer is threefold. First, there is the independent force of life that she bears upon herself. The fact that Jews can still spread themselves out so unshakably throughout the world can be explained by this effect. As deep as the exhaustion may be, exhaustion by which generation after generation of men is worn out by the battle of life, the woman—less strained spiritually, less worn down by studying and by the sleeplessness of study, more subdued and more down to earth in her spirit and her imagination, much more purely given to the general feminine instincts—has always been capable of compensating for the loss. And thanks to her unrestrained temperament, she has been capable of stating everything as it is, of repelling and rendering harmless all that only she would be able to undermine, all that becomes repressed or festers in her. Second, there is the deep, grateful loyalty with which her husband remains continually devoted to her. The Jewish woman of the people need fear less than any other bride that a rival could emerge; here the discipline of Jewish

antisexual ethics has created something so positive that along with it, one has to accept indiscriminately its antisocial shadow. The loyalty of the Jew, the unswerving focus on the decision that has been made and into which he has entered, is an almost dictated connection among human being, law, and tradition, indeed a cardinal attribute of the people. It is not a gloomy, lethargic state of stagnation, but a constantly renewed motion that, as in all central relations of the Jews, including marriage, breeds this fidelity.

It is only natural that in such a taxing and woeful life strife and squabbles occur among married couples; however, physical abuse does not occur, or only as something out of the ordinary. The Jewish woman does not have that peculiar pride in being dominated by a combative and manly husband that allows him to express his love through abuse and a strict regimen, just as she is missing the desire for the slave-holding tests of a particular kind of woman. In both cases, there is a deep respect for the divine creation that human life presents. Here the holy observance of the bond between two people through the sacrament of marriage is not an empty formula, not a false pretext . . . And the third form of support is the great respect and love of the children toward their parents. It seems that in our generation the alienation of the young from the old is very apparent. Yet even in this state of war, in the way in which it is experienced by the children, without rawness and as a matter of bitter necessity, there lies an entirely different kind of inner warmth than that which is experienced by other people in the same conditions and of the same class background. The independence of Jewish children has, in certain respects, more free play than that of others. They can be quite sure of being supported in their engagement in spiritual activity, in school, in opportunities for study, with all the means—indeed, beyond all the means—at their parents' disposal. Thus, they remain responsible for matters concerning the maintenance of the lives of their parents longer than other young people would, and only recently have sons been able to enter into marriage without being dependent upon parental approval of the choice— never mind daughters. Between the two generations there is a tacit connection to the mutual responsibility for the third, for the task of the Jewish spirit to persevere. And among the children there is, above all, the acknowledgment of the unremitting effort, the noble sacrifice, the selflessness of their parents. That's why the mother is often an idol for the sons, for in the twilight of her life she is honored and cared for as well as is humanly possible within the power of her children. She is fortunate . . .

In the course of life her relationship to fortune is certainly unusual. The mindset of the Jew is anything but blissfully happy; the goal of being happy in life does not exist for him. When it says in the fifth commandment, "Honor thy father and thy mother, so that you may live long in the land," the "so that" is neither a reason nor a reward for the fulfillment of the commandment, but rather a *conditio sine qua non:* without honoring your parents, you cannot fare well, without them, you have no continued existence. But you will live, and live long, if you live according to the will of the pious work that is given to you. Thus, constant resignation encompasses the life of the Jew, and even more the life of the Jewish woman from the people. For naturally she approaches life with the rich, happy dreams of a child's imagination; naturally she too hopes for a miracle. And then the wretched reality takes hold such that she quickly learns to bow her head in despair, her chin sinks upon her breast, her mouth drops down painfully, her forehead wrinkles . . . "So that you live long in the land which the Lord, your God, has given unto you." Has the yearning of a landless people ever been more deeply interwoven in human relations than it is here? And has long life—not light and blessed life—ever been so highly regarded as a value as it is here? One might imagine for a moment this type of human being next to the Homeric-Sophoclean: "[T]he second best is to die young, the best, however, is not to be born." One might compare the life of the ancient Greek with that of the ancient Jew—the radiant with the harsh—and one would see two heroes next to each other, the one with a raging will for freedom, who would rather perish than suffer, and the other with an urgent sense of duty, who would rather suffer through everything than perish. If the Jew

were oriented toward fortune, he would long ago have been wiped out of existence. This principle is preserved in each individual. And the strange thing about this is that the lack of good fortune does not embitter the Jew; it makes him neither morose nor reproachful or envious. Rather, he is filled with a resolute composure toward that which is given to him—the determined efficiency of the human being who is capable of fulfilling a God-given mission with limitless joy. Just wait, young woman, in your state of disappointment: you will soon feel that even pleasure flows toward this real, un-dreamed-of existence; your head will soon lift itself and your mouth will learn how to smile about the same incidents that currently aggravate you. That is God's solace given to the active soul.

But it is very necessary for her, since naturally this whole perspective is only valid if one looks at the facts from very high up and with the salvation of all in one's heart. The individual, the woman considered in and of herself, the single marriage viewed at close range, all reveal a much more complex and difficult external manifestation. Without scruples and frictions, without painful and dangerous inflammation, neither the consummation of a marriage of such an impersonal kind nor the development of marriage itself can be carried out. Erotic problems exist everywhere, and the higher one climbs the social ladder, the more enlightened one's consciousness, the more serious a fate they commonly seem to be. In such a synthetic overview as this book, one can cling to all the shortcomings of one's subject, but one can only point to the particulars and talk about this problem briefly.

The Jewish woman is weighed down, more heavily than other women, by the enormous pressure of centuries-old erotic, antierotic guidance. From the start, she is missing self-confidence in the possibility of enduring every feminine fate. Her instincts, which otherwise secure her, are abandoned as soon as she is in love. Nobody is as easily deceived as she, who trusts so infinitely; she knows this, and that is why she is so suspicious, insecure, anxious, awkward. In addition, there is a deep, diffident fear of gaining happiness from strong sensual inclinations, a nervous system that is easily brought to terror by erotic circumstances, and a strongly emphasized tendency toward intellectuality, toward brooding, which is often missing in the balance within the harmless, natural, body-affirming realm. Thus, one should not be surprised if the sharpest arc in the life of the Eastern Jewish woman is defined precisely at this point, one at which she can easily be derailed: the result of frigidity, repulsion toward her husband, salvation from her child or from physical and mental disorder. One might also consider the fact that the young Jewish soul who is deprived of every facet of an erotic culture, indeed, of a culture of love, and who is left to his own taboo-consumed instincts is capable of committing the gruff and careless blunders that one otherwise avoids through lovingly acquired tact, education, and self-cultivation—that is, if they are not replaced with the gruffness of the clueless. And finally, one might consider the fact that if one takes a look at the more advanced Jewish sectors than those hitherto examined, marriages that are consummated without love only succeed those sectors in which it is not individuals but man and wife as such who are erotically unified. This case no longer corresponds to the Jew of a higher bourgeois class; at least the woman is often a more differentiated human type than the man, who in a vital sense is commonly disfigured and nearly dehumanized by his work or study, whereas the woman approaches him still entirely preserved and with immensely strict and barely damaged discipline. The woman thus suffers occasionally from disappointments of immeasurable depth, shocks, and nervous breakdowns. She reaches the point of finding her spouse loathsome. Perhaps for her, the topic of sexuality remains delicate, something dirty, only tolerable for the sake of children. Apart from very difficult, rare cases, there are two general consequences: either the well-to-do woman, dissatisfied by the reality of marriage, takes advantage of her devotion to an idea—either in a passive sense, in which she "educates herself," or more actively, as a member of a practical organization or a political party; or the immense, human-driving force of habit, of no longer being capable of surprise, gives her a normalizing perspective toward the humane value of her spouse, toward the virtue and duty of the home and love for her children as the real purpose of marriage—and this

gradually makes the marriage ugly. In fact, the nerves of children of such marriages remain vulnerable enough, but in the end, enthusiastic devotion to and care for the young brood by the mother and the fantastic physical and spiritual force of the race, of the people, usually break through that which was initially poorly done, and they stabilize at once the wife, the home, the marriage, and the child. In this regard, a "good marriage" of this kind is erotically tepid, which applies to the bulk of affluent Jews one meets: there is mutual warm admiration of the parents for each other, and as for the value of family (of raising children), they are nearly at a first-class rate in our time.

IV.

In such a home, in this air and this environment, youth grows up.

It is difficult, from a standpoint of calm detachment, to make sense of the silent faces of these young human beings, which, despite the natural sincerity of their people, only give away what they wish to say or what on occasion exposes itself—or to guess the movements, the currents, and turmoil that pulls them in a direction in which we cannot look. And if anywhere, it should be said here that this book is not supported by specialized literature, not by reports, but rather merely by the present condition of life and by the spiritual gift of observing. It is as wrong or right as the configuration itself which life presents to the observer. Hence the gaps, hence the exaggerations: it is a testimony. Youth, however, is bashful, and Jewish youth is three times as bashful toward Western Jews, whose pitying arrogance, shown during visits to their Eastern Jewish "relatives," is not capable of facilitating warmth, fairness, and familiarity. Before one strikes up a friendship, the moment has passed. And to the first general remark, a second one might be linked: movements among the young are not strictly differentiated according to sex. The same forces affect boys and girls. Even if answers and reactions are separated by sex, we may be permitted to describe just one, the characteristic mode of reacting. The reader may be willing enough to ask for himself—and to answer, if he can—the question of how well the other sex may react toward the same forces and the same conditions.

We did not recognize everyday life, did not see the peaceful street in the evening, we do not know how the young girl sees her life and how she led it when the young men were still all at home, before the time when legions of soldiers broke all previous codes and instituted new ones—when German officers, with a clatter of spurs and blinded by arrogance, hadn't yet advanced their course. The average Russian soldier was hardly noticed and the Russian officer was a friendly foreigner, very humane, very civilized and educated. He knew a bit about the great empire and his interaction was pleasant and harmless, like any interaction between a foreigner and a Jewish woman. The ancient practice of preserving the tribe was not difficult for her and, with rare exception, romantic relationships existed only between young Jews.

Indeed, we know from the sweet and naive Jewish folk love song that youth enters into liaisons like any other tender, rapturous, and resolute contacts between the new, high feeling and its sought-after destiny, perhaps sometimes more hesitantly than with simpler kinds of people, and without final union; and then tragedy, youthful tragedy ensues when irrational beauty blows rational life off course . . . But that is the case with all people: love songs tap into the vital feeling of youth, its fortune and its sorrow, and behind them lies the humble compromise. Friendship, flame, youthful eroticism, and flirtation or even love should not, by a long shot, have played the role they play in the West. It is widely known that the war ushered in harmful forces in all regions. For although the Jewish small town was never entirely spared from affliction, such an inhumane, repressive, devastating affliction as the one that has dominated in the cities—those that were hermetically cut off from the supplies around them—first as a result of the Russian then of the German war measures, has in peacetime only existed in the most dreadful centers of Indian famine. All around, the fields, pastures, and trees bore rich crops. But the Jews, whose craftsmanship and labor, trade and professions were ravaged by the confiscation of all raw materials and machines, by the requisitioning of apartments and stores, by the flight of almost the entire constituency of well-to-do industrialists and buyers, and by the ruin of those who remained, were almost fully shut down. Their monetary means were even more radically damaged by the political and official exchange rate of the ruble. The Jews suddenly saw themselves with official rations whose limits on foodstuffs, set in Germany, made the rations blatantly insufficient and often of an almost inedible quality, handed out by an army of men who had long been without women and who at every chance offered food and relief in exchange for sexual favors. When considered from this point of view, and from that of the widespread raging dysentery and typhus epidemic—the result of excessive consumption of fruit—which appeared to quash the continuation of every life and the continuation of its moral effect, the destructive influence of the army on Jewish women's morality remains quite low.

In the wide eyes of these girls you see the innocent tranquility, the trusting nature of organic creatures who gladly exchange a word with humans, because humans are created in God's image, and friendliness is their commandment; who withdraw, disconcerted and wounded, when the Westerner, the shoddy psychologist, claims that there is an erotic feeling at play here and then maintains that he is witnessing a kind of cryptic flirtatiousness. Look at these innocent, full lips that are nothing more than childlike, whereas the European raised on the catchwords of operettas thinks he is discerning sensuality and who knows what else, anticipating the mass-produced kitsch fantasies to which the Jewish woman is subjected: that racial traits such as dark eyes and black hair, whose bearers may be pure as Luna, cannot prevent either soldier or student from wanting to make love to a dusky female Jew, Pole, or Spaniard. Not all girls have the sensitivity of their souls written across their mouths or on their parted lips; rarely does melancholy stand plainly between their curved eyebrows, and the pointed oval of their face, in its outline, does not often tremble from alienation so expressively as in these days. And indeed from our standpoint, we have seen so much melancholy in the existence of these poor and simple Jewish daughters, who blossom without

blossoming, squat, timid, and in semi-darkness, whose girlish smile is entirely the smile of a child and never receives the satiated and triumphant shine of the power of Eros and the forceful, instinctual self-awareness of a woman who can choose among her suitors and snatch victory away from one of them.

Do they then marry? No, marriage is arranged without real consideration for individual love. Instead, they enter into a poor, humanly adequate, and tender relationship without the "passion" about which they have occasionally read, into a marriage filled with worries and culminating in many children, from which their own youth retreats quickly, imperceptibly, resigned. That such a life, which otherwise appears so melancholy, can be led and fulfilled in an entirely happy way, that there can even be a lively cheeriness full of conversation and celebration, becomes self-evident. The gift of coming to terms with life so resolutely, the efficient art of accepting it however it falls, of never despairing at any hour, and of cherishing the unremitting hope for better times—this feminine "virtue" among Jewish women is presumably the primary source of their continuously successful tenacity. This race, whose men abuse themselves in drudgery, would be unthinkable if not for this sheer power of innocence and rejuvenation at work in its mothers—contributing toward our salvation.

The Jewish woman, with a child in her arms, reveals the most well rounded character of the East. Only the old man, with the Torah scrolls in his arms or holding a book in both hands, is comparable to her. The shawl, draped from her shoulders and wrapped around the small creature, does not cover the child more warmly or more fully than the expression that she casts from beneath her eyelashes. She is, at this point, no longer worthy of adornment herself; her hair, strictly hidden beneath an artificial wig, denies her entire feminine desire to be beautiful. Just as honest and strong as her face is, so too is her concern about this pledge to the future. Yet the intensity with which she observes her pledge has nothing brutish about it, for she must work tirelessly to come to terms with all that is supported by her: small business, home, children, worries.

We soldiers have witnessed this kind of life in excess: how the husband looks to earn his daily bread outside of the home; how he tries to search for goods, to find customers, to make his skills marketable; how he suspiciously pursues and inquires about the political scene and its influence on the earnings of tomorrow; how he seeks a respite and escape in the Hebrew-printed book. And yet at home the wife is all in one: she sells the goods from the small shop, keeps the records, examines banknotes while she fetches groceries, prepares the meals, always back and forth between the shop and the kitchen, from the study to the courtyard in which the children play. Cleanliness, order, and comfort are almost impossible to produce in these dreadful poverty-stricken and cramped conditions— and yet despite all the hustle and bustle and the general plight, only seldom does she show a quarrelsome or fierce side . . . There is no longer the world of books, for the world of faith has become practical and is dictated according to the law of food. She learned how to care for children when she herself was a child and had to cater to the youngest and to look after her—she does not know that she is a hero and she would laugh if we told her so. To her, life has left only the simplest of problems: to see to it that her husband should be kind, that one should get enough to eat today and hopefully tomorrow as well, and that nothing bad, God forbid, should happen to her child. And yet what this kind of existence holds over similar kinds is that it is natural without ever being rough or vulgar. A humankind, a motherhood of infallible constitution, reveals itself in this humble being. Taking out one's anger, disappointment, and nervousness on one's children, beating them or shouting at them brutally, becoming greedy, indifferent, and envious in one's words and thoughts: such responses, produced by poverty, are rarely found here. Even with youth snatched away by woes, she tries to preserve childhood for the children. Thus she unconsciously holds the most important task high above herself: to save for these new beings, beings that she herself produces without becoming a victim, a fresh, unsullied, unencumbered beginning, and she does so with the sureness in her heart that children are a blessing, the blessing of the Lord—a blessing filled with worries, a burden which even in doubtful times she carries and makes better. Young Jewish girl . . . she does not know that she is our ancestral mother Leah, again at work for the people . . .

Girls who do not marry are uncommon, so we are told. We who are bound to the superficial are only capable of following individual lives for a short period of time; then we leave the site and only the thoughts remain. But we saw the beginning of such paths of life from which it would be odd if they were to end any differently than in the impenetrable depths of Warsaw or Vilna. They are the girls who all too happily listened to the songs that spoke of handsome students and soldiers. Helpless in the face of rising prices, they have sought the protection of a soldier who receives bread and meat. This path leads to a tearoom, of which there are thousands of harmless kinds and a few dangerous ones as well, and ends perhaps in a typhus fever infirmary, or in one of the bordellos that the military government has set up separately for officers, sergeants, and servicemen—a terrible bunch of the most debased sort seeking to relieve their needs—until she is led into a fenced-in building or into one of the courtyards in which "prostitutes" are "healed" of their occupational ailments.

Her enticing glance, her beautifully opened mouth, and the low, foolhardy forehead of a young girl can indeed seal her fate. Perhaps the simple lifting of her eyebrows may, in this magnificent culture, suggest a quick detour into the Hotel Katherina. Such a precious, long, oval face, a small nose and dainty nostrils, can give the impression that a girl resolutely rejects manual labor, that she intensifies her instincts toward flirtatiousness, and, as the victim and symbol of our European situation, she allows herself to make a living from the one urge that mows down civilization everywhere, lifting her innocence toward ethical indifference. However, her life can take an altogether different course: perhaps she conceives a child, and her child dies—how often this occurs in dire times! The pain and all this knocking about instills in her an aversion toward new relations. She thus enters a house as a young maid, and all her splendid instincts can blossom: work, care, and the most delightful innate sense of wit . . .

for that which perishes in the human being is indeed so inexpressibly little. Unneeded or unwelcome, it can remain dormant for decades. One can forget, forget entirely, how successful this laughter or work once was. But the human being does not change itself, only its face, turned by the outside world toward the customs of the day. And because this face is formed by one's environment and occupation, necessity and coincidence, not conditioned primarily by the soul, it is absurd to attribute the attitudes of such a professional face *[Berufsgesicht]* to the soul of the human being. No, it is not the forsaken human being that walks up to you. It is the professional face of the prostitute, it is the wretched, filthy, abject environment of the prostitute that you find so vulgar and you detest inexpressibly. She herself is it, the human being is unalterably bound to its essences and like the shape of a well-formed eye, it is separate from the filth in which you now encounter it or into which you see it sinking. That is why the face of the dead prostitute is as pure as a girl's face . . . It is not death that stands majestically above it. Only the environment, the loathsome life did death cast aside like a straggly gray hair . . .

At the very moment in which an upper school is opened there begins a problem that is no longer an individual one, but rather the principal problem of youth. School in general is not the starting point about which I am writing here. School is of course a starting point. Eyes that are able to read see the world more fully than those that cannot. The hand that is able to write is a different hand from that which is not. It is not that we should partake of the nonsense in which one rates a culture higher or lower according to its number of illiterates. The decisive factor alone remains the ethical quality of the human being, and the progress is such that culture, soul, and a helpful disposition can have greater effect among the illiterates than among the learned of advanced capitalism, those of scientific warfare and its blissful centralization. But apart from coincidental developments—and in view of the real phenomena—the writing hand of the human being reveals itself as that which is armed with the key to all spiritual riches, to the past and the future. The human being that can inform itself is no longer helpless . . . But the general school of the Jewish people does not present the problem of acquiring knowledge as the most urgent and complex problem about which one needs to talk.

The entire stiflingly protective nature of a people is rallied around this young girl who is writing. Her childlike neck cannot support a head filled with skepticism, her chin promises the fruitful inertia of her small skull; her mouth seeks neither words of denial nor new gospels. Her arm, which lies stationary upon the table, is still, in its state of restfulness, an impatient and active arm which would rather knead dough, sweep up, or hold children; and her hand is coarse and strong, awkward while writing, agile and happy while lighting candles or drawing water. Presumably, this girl's mind is more alert and quicker than that of girls of the same kind and class in other cultures. Yet that is merely a national difference and not a threat. Would it be desirable to get rid of the danger once and for all, to dull the Jewish genius and thereby gain security? Never. No other people has a continued existence more endangered than that of the Jewish people, but ethnic groups have no means of retreating, and with the growth of the danger also comes the growth of salvation.

The danger begins with those young people to whom the riches of the world are revealed. A youth movement of the kind that is in Germany does not exist among the Jews of the East. One must invite and support the German model, for its noble goals are innocuous. It reveals sources to the German soul, renews its spirit and leads with a kind of natural feeling toward German tradition. The best of German youth wishes to liberate the German soul from its bourgeois displacement; it leads to the finest form of national tradition.

The strongest movement among Eastern Jewish youth has disproportionately more serious names than "youth movement." It is called Socialism or revolution. It negates Jewish tradition, indeed, departs from it altogether, consciously and systematically; it tosses away every particular mode of being in favor of the general mold of the Russian human being. For the Eastern Jew, this movement has a name which is also familiar to the Western Jew: assimilation. Yet if assimilation in the West is watered down, bourgeois, second-rate, and "liberal," if the assimilated

circles of youth—exceptions not addressed now—distinguish themselves by their total lack of significance, lack of ideals, and their pragmatic and feeble phraseology, if it is the oddest union of theory and pomposity out of which only a vast mediocrity is produced, in the East assimilation is at once more revolutionary, radical, ready for action, and promoted by the most valuable and powerful kinds of people. The Jewish spirit becomes less impoverished in Western assimilation; Judaism becomes more impoverished in Eastern assimilation. All contradictions, which youth can experience within itself, flow in one and the same direction, all energies, which youth feels alive within itself, drive toward the same goal.

The degree to which Eastern youth participates in the political being of the general public is for the moment unimaginable to the Westerner. Indeed, here in the West one assumes that the youth should study and thus should not be concerned with politics. Very well. If a country stagnates politically as much as the former German empire, in which all real political decisions were glossed by a false parliament, never coming into being by popular decree, and in which the people, outside the "revolutionary" parties, approve of this condition because politics would only destroy its business, then it contents itself only in a feeble way with party affiliation and kindles in its heart no ideals of communal being whatsoever. In Germany, the authoritarian state was supported and exploited by its subject, the people, while in the Russian empire it was negated and fought against. The ideals of human freedom and participation reign among the pupils of the upper schools, and they are central issues among the students. How can one go on studying when the spirit is subjugated and persecuted? How can one merely have one's career in mind while the people are nervous and are being shaken by the demons of social welfare? That would be the case, if not for the youth that is so capable. In addition to that, there is the firm solidarity of the proletarianized people whose mouth, spirit, and blood constitute the Russian intelligentsia, which is aligned with the oppressed, cooped-up, and threatened people at the margins, "foreign peoples" of the empire, all of whom suffer in the exact same way from a deprivation of rights, and the firm solidarity of the bourgeoisie with the people against the system—a unified community in battle *[Kampfgemeinschaft]* leading up to the overthrow of the system, an apparent contradiction only in this regard. In spite of her gentle face and mild gaze, the smiling, coddled daughter of the Jewish bourgeoisie is in fact a devotee of the struggle of the worker. Underneath her forehead, crowned with rich, well-coiffed hair, the ideas of Krapotkin and the role model of Tolstoy are at work. And so the whips of the Cossacks crack, which disperses the revolutionary masses, reaching all the cities of western Russia and the backs and heads of the schoolchildren, as the Cossack horses turn against them, and the police prisons thus become filled with "Gymnasiskes" [high school pupils] and with workers. (In fact, in the school system, girls were not kept apart from boys; there was only "youth.") Still living in their memory of those days in 1905 and 1906, their eyes are filled with sparkle and spite, and in the paralyzed, occupied zone, underneath the frozen surface, every push forward from the revolution of 1917 on is at work in the hearts of the youth.

Then of course, in 1907, after the bloody suppression of the uprisings, an almost indescribable wave of despair descended upon the youth. Since the reigning regime still maintained power, despite having lost its battle with Japan, the wish to take on the role of master via the popular movement—was it not unshakable? So it seemed: life no longer had any value. Striving, wanting, hoping, all of which pointed toward forward movement, appeared to be cut off; self-sacrifice, courage, the will to act appeared senseless. Never, even on the most inauspicious of occasions, did young people give themselves over to death more easily, and among the survivors, in the years 1907 and 1908, there prevailed the spirit of "après nous le déluge." Only enjoyment of the present moment seemed to have a purpose. As a means of anesthetization, drinking from all cups of life was the only alternative left to a youth whose ideals had melted away. Of all the impulses that guide the youth, only that aimed at existential beauty, at tenderness and physical intimacy, appeared unbroken. As a result, in the realm of sensuousness, this motive took from such

haunted and wildly destroyed hope the most crazed of paths. Out of the secret political organizations and circles among male and female students there arose "Leagues of Free Love" in which wine and brandy appeared on the tables during truly despairing discussions held with the lights turned off. Disillusioned to the core, the youth drove itself full force into a frenzy of self-destruction. The novel *Ssasin*, an unimportant and largely ignored book in the West, depicted this atmosphere: in it the youth recognized itself and reflected upon itself—and that accorded the work its Russian success. For if anything could follow the cresting wave of disillusionment, it would be the hope slowly surging in and the unequivocal decision to make a new attempt. At this moment, the revolution had already triumphed: its sincerity, fueled by the indestructible will of the people to live humanely, had redeemed it.

All forces that drive this youth toward revolution work centrifugally, spinning outward from Jewish tradition. This is solely and exclusively the consequence of our stateless, landless existence. The Russian Revolution changes Russian tradition, but it doesn't dissolve it; revolutionized German youth, if it were to exist, would give the German essence a new breakthrough. Both may be as internationally oriented, or better yet, cosmopolitan, as they wish, but they bear the national color of their being, even in the quickest advances into the future. The Jewish youth, however, as a Jewish people, comes to an end (there are exceptions; more about that soon). These forces affect not one's own conditions, but rather, in the desire to affect the general public, external conditions; the effect is anti-Jewish. These are forces that grow in the essence of youth itself, forces that exist everywhere, except with us; they have a socially destructive side effect, one that impoverishes the Jewish spirit. This is an established fact and not a value judgment. What is depraved is the terribly disadvantaged condition of Jewish tradition, not Jewish youth, which has no choice but to follow its impulses.

Let us take, for example, a girl of the educated class, whose face expresses most strongly the average of her kind, the vitality of the people. Not a single feature of her face has been shaped by individual fate, but

instead all distinctive marks of national belonging are most clearly stamped upon her. And so too was her spirit created, her temperament, her will and feeling; she is created in the image of her grandmother, exponentially raised into the typical. Such a girl of German or Russian extraction and part of a revolutionary generation will constitute the most vital factor in the continued existence of a nation that there is: she represents national tradition in the face of the future. A Jewish girl of this kind, born in the East, has all the prospects of bringing Jewish virtues to Latvian, Russian, Ukrainian, or Polish national tradition, insofar as she devotes herself to the revolutionary cause. This is the condition of the Jewish people, a people on whose continued existence depends more than on the existence of Polish tradition or of Latvian spirit. What becomes impoverished are among the best fruits of its precious seeds.

Because the revolutionary instincts of Jewish youth find no countersupport in the otherwise innate reality of social isolation, because the Jewish people is only defined according to blood and has no geographic borders, because its revolution—only co-conceived, silently as it were, and not clearly recognizable—can only direct itself against the scruples, vices, and sins of its own people, all of this is why, everywhere beyond its beginnings, Jewish revolution gives rise to the regressive turn toward such toxic and bitter byproducts as rampant bourgeois antisemitism. The only kind of revolution that is truly legitimate, however, is the kind that is like a human being who beats his own breast and announces his own guilt.

The immediate rejection by the youth applies to the home of the parents, as to the family. This is entirely justified during times of spiritual renewal, when the older generation—unaware of the fact that its stance is spiritually frozen and that, in spite of the noble truthfulness of many individuals, it no longer acts like a generation in active devotion to the rights and duties of human beings on earth, but in traditional, categorical attention to rules—wishes naively to impose upon its children its way of living. Even if these children don't know exactly where they wish to go, at least they know, with overwhelming clarity, what they wish to get away from. An immeasurable revulsion startles them at the thought that

Tevye?

they could become like those who have produced such horror: cold, detached, and spiteful, daughters turn their faces away from the mode of existence of their mothers, whose physical appearance they can no longer bear, especially when they fear that they see their own future in it. Get away, simply get away! Better to end poorly in the unknown than to continue to tolerate what is known to be wretched. That is why what is foreign for them, in terms of value, is that which does not remind them of home. Sons feel this, if it is at all possible, even more viscerally.

Work and relaxation, contact and leisure, social interaction and solitude have their own rhythm among the young, and because compromise is considered a slap in the face, they have to attempt to maintain this rhythm in place of that of their parents. The less that customs and financial conditions allow for separation, the more fiercely the grievousness grows rampant. Their parents' work strikes the youth as haggling, their relaxation as deadly distraction, their human contact as unbearably petit bourgeois, their lifestyle as appalling hypocrisy, their social interaction as gossip and chatter and ridiculous card games, or, if Sabbath strolls and theater visits are passed off as experiences with nature and the arts, they smack of vile profanity and abused holy traditions. Above all, youths rebel against the constant compulsion to appear in public with those deemed unwanted, and thus see themselves as abused by their families. A person who is not capable of being alone, who every now and then does not have the need to be alone with himself, is for the young person less worthy than a table or a door. Included among these rejected and despised conditions of family existence is the condition of being Jewish—an aura, a cast of mind, a custom apart from the cultic and religious.

Jewish is the Sabbath, Jewish are the holidays and the customary dishes, language, books, ancestors, laws of merit according to which one forms values, and instincts according to which one affirms and negates. Jewish are jokes and gestures, linguistic irregularities and bodily shapes, individual affliction and moral prejudices. All this is Jewish or "Jewish." But the family is the only true national manifestation, the national type, the manifestation of human existence. And just as this family is affected by the full force of youthful condemnation, so too, among Jews, is the central artery of their national existence. Human existence, nothing more, is the watchword of national hemorrhage. And wherever one recognizes that one would not be capable of being a human any differently than by giving oneself over, as one's only means, to the national cause, one chooses the boundless, glorious, and entirely lively Russian tradition. Young girl, daughter, you shake your curls and carry your well-rounded profile, cool eyes, trembling nose, proud narrow mouth, and trustworthy chin toward the other national tradition without knowing what you are giving away here—you do not know how Jewish you behave . . .

Youth—good youth—also condemns, in this senseless and irreverent time, the religion it was taught. It knows precisely that if only that which takes place in temples and in mumbled prayers, in laws and rituals, should be religion, then it is dead, and if only that which wishes to be worshiped this way is God, then he is dead three times over. Nietzsche's proclamation of the death of God is better understood, better heard, than Amos' proclamation of God's will. (Western Jewish soldiers stationed in Eastern Jewish big cities had to bring to life, for the enlightened youth, the psalms and the prophets for the first time . . .) The soul of the youth is full of longing for worship and spirit; their big eyes, opened wide, seek it out; their necks lift their heavy, doubt-ridden heads so that they can look into the distance and catch sight of the new faith to which their mouths, soft and yearning, are ready to bear witness. But that which one claims to believe and for which one requires faith, devotion, and worship, that which professes to be the connection to the essence of the world and of life—that is an annoying ringing bell for the youth. The youth has to serve God while creating for itself a new God, a God that is true. From the most malicious of doubts to the most radical condemnations, it has to put to a halt every kind of ridicule. It has to wrestle with God and around God, to find peace with the "God of the Fathers"—to keep youth from terrible, tragic disorientation! For the God of the youth has a veiled face [*Antlitz*], but once the youth has learned how to imagine this face, then it is there. Yet, the God of the fathers, the religion of Jewish

revelation, is now just the form and limit of Jewish existence vis-à-vis the non-Jewish world. And insofar as the youth no longer respects this limit, as atheistic as it may feel, it throws itself into the rocking sphere of non-Judaism, this sea of time, like a detached, redeemed dirt clod from a disappearing island.

Youth—good youth—hates money. It sees that the old people would not be who they are today if money, property, investment, and return were not the only weapons in the inhumane battle of the anti-Jewish and capitalist versus the Jews in this stateless and deprived present, the only weapons that one allowed them, that one could take with one everywhere one went when, as a result of boycott, decree, or war, one was forced to flee. These weapons are demons, useful but paid for at a high price, which makes their souls evaporate and only allows them one way to make up for it, the automaton, the golem, the capitalist bourgeois. Indeed, youth hates money, but it scorns it even more and scorns terribly its slaves, unfortunate products of the nineteenth century whose lives are realized in "earning money," making a means of life into their sole purpose, with such singlemindedness! To tremble about one's earnings? To beg for, express thanks, and worry about one's earnings? To calculate, even in one's sleep, and at every waking moment, how to take advantage of one's service to the terrible machine that is called "business"? Not to pay heed to any real leisure nor to any joy that is not bought; to see nature as a business object (raw material) and the human being as life material (work force); to see in the non-commercial artist and in the perceptive, critical, demon-lacerating poet harmless, odd gypsies, and to grant respect according to financial possessions and to rank honor in the world along those lines—what would youth be, if it did not stand up against that! But money is now the only weapon and the only force of the present-day bourgeois Jew. It is for him the only way to secure his political place in life, and insofar as the youth has fought with all its might against money, it has threatened the foundation of the current Jewish bourgeois existence.

And quite pervasively and quite brusquely, youth, good youth rejects the milieu in which it grew up. These people with their small-minded thoughts from whom one always hears the same words, the same into-nations—how ridiculous they are, how remarkably stupid is their gait! These streets, how revoltingly passé, these coffeehouses, how monoto-nous, these gardens, how dead and how overfilled with wretched people! This environment, how foul! A boundless yearning cries out: away from here! Into the free air, the vastness, the unknown, the freshly created! There is the true life, here merely its phantom; there is power, courage, and a wide horizon, here a dead end whose gutter stinks. The youth goes off and rejoices, and with each visit to the city of childhood, that city ap-pears shabbier and stranger—and before it can become touching and holy, it is forgotten, or the youth is no longer young and is firmly entrenched in life elsewhere. And yet the city of childhood is the only place to which the Jew can attach his joyful home-seeking heart. The flight from this environment, often viewed principally in a youthful vein, becomes a flight into foreign, metropolitan, diffuse de-Jewification *[Entjudung]*.

Thus, all instincts of repulsion drive entire packs of youths away from Judaism. They repress their positive attributes, even if these are no real special scientific or artistic gifts, they allow the human beings, who are totally absorbed by this, no other choice than their education and striv-ing toward Socialism.

Youth—good youth—must admire somebody, or it cannot exist. And what good fortune, if in this era there are men and women whose shin-ing bravery, whose dedication and courage to sacrifice, whose helpful-ness and comradeship serve as a model, an impetus, and an enticing goal to achieve! Jewish youth should not acknowledge greatness and heroism in the service of violence and conquest, of war and destruction, but only in the service of ideas and freedom, of reconstruction and humanity. And that is why the revolutionaries of the long battle for human rights and a dignified life on earth, who fight their battle in Russia, have much greater effect than the uniformed soldier-heroes of the West, than the conquerors and explorers whose aftereffects were slavery, murder, rapacity, and in-

justices of every kind. They are stronger than the historical, now shadowy, and unimaginable Maccabeans, stronger than the martyrs and passive heroes of Judaism whose ideology one can no longer feel—all the
people murdered, missing in prisons, those who were banished and those
who fled, all the perpetrators of these deeds with word and weapon.

And if a girl with a calm and pure face, with a high forehead and wide
temples, with a discreet mouth and straight neck saw all the images of
Socialist female students, the calm and pure faces, high foreheads and
discreet mouths—would not the decision to live this way then flare up
within her heart: I too solemnly swear to be like this, I too am capable?
Examples will inspire the succession of youth wherever youth is of a pure
and determined will, and people cannot sink much lower than those
whose sons and daughters, totally devoid of any instinct to serve the youth
in the process of rejuvenation, band together in the preservation of the
existing structure and in support of the powers that be.

A burning sense of justice flows in the heart of the youth, of good
youth. For to approve of the horrible injustice of the godforsaken life in
modern times, to exploit it—a people could not sink much lower than
this. And so Jewish youth joins in the outcry for social justice that is called
Socialism, and it wants it all. It wants to engage in it in order to bring
about fulfillment. According to its idea, if nature is unjust, then humanity must assert its idea of justice as a counterbalance all the more vocif-
erously! If human nature is such that the strong subjugate the weak, then
all the more profound is the duty of humankind to rush to the aid of the
weak. Who am I to say that I should own more than you? Let us share.
Nobody requires more than is necessary, and how rich the earth is for
fair distribution, how little the human being needs in order to live happily! For the non-Jew, "justice," which is capable of overwhelming the
Jew, appears to be almost inconceivable as an essential notion. It is a pe-
culiarity for a person who has the cold, barren, jealous Roman conception of justice in his blood. The warmth that radiates from justice, the
flame with which it asserts itself in the Jew, who sees in it the regulative
mode of life par excellence, the grand vision of the self-governing and

mediating world—all this surges up in Jewish youth when it yearns for Socialism. As do all the other affirming forces of good youth: for the Jew, who experiences them in a special way, in a Jewish way, they all flow into Socialism. There is the drive toward comradeship, toward benevolence, the same drive that Jews have exerted since they first wandered the earth and without which the Jews would no longer be here. This drive locates its immediate goal in the comrade-in-arms, its most distant in the deprived troops of people. This is the battle instinct of youth, an instinct transformed by the Jews into spirit, which is aimed against the biggest monster, autocratic capitalism, an opponent worth fighting against. The real starting points for imagining the work of the spirit and work of the hands in the very facts of life are the active instinct of youth, which must be deployed against the resistance and for the realization which only really exists in the act that is carried out, and the creative instinct, which is the youth itself, the beginning of an existence.

Consider here the young Jew, with his many years of schooling, from a bourgeois home. Look at his sunken shoulders and his slight figure, his clever eyes above his cunning mouth; look, as it is captured in his profile, at his weakness and his unbreakable courage, his awkward gait and his pensive spite; he still dons the cap of a high school student and carries his books under his arm, but he is already a Socialist. Thus, although looked at disparagingly, he will strengthen his knowledge at your universities, he will show up at your meetings and with his name, and especially with his words, he will provoke your darkest instincts. He will tell your workers what there is to be done and he will do it—whether right or wrong, he will do it completely—and he will thus stand before your drumhead court-martial and be killed by your soldiers, soldiers who will never know what they are doing. Or he shall triumph.

For he affirms his innermost essence when he is a Socialist. Only a Jew can gauge the vastness of the waste that the capitalist has created, as he is part of a people born into the proletariat of pharaoh's absolutism and oppressed to the point that justice became its innermost core. Guided

by the spirit of a lawmaker into whom God himself hammered the primal words of humanity and dominated for centuries by his primal figure, spread out across the beautiful and blessed land by legitimate order and repeatedly chased into line, from the innate human waste leading toward egocentrism and hunger for power, by the prophets, they are God's glorious shepherds. A people that more than once gave birth to the pure, spiritual, loving human being in order to sort out the world that was not capable of stopping him—in terms of human type a mystery to the genius of love, conceivable for others only as the innate son of God, so nonhuman this purity appeared to them. A people crushed by the Romans, tortured to the utmost extreme by a thousand large or small perpetrators of violence—for who was so weak as not to be capable of committing violence to the Jew? A people, this people, still here, still young, carrying on as on its first day. Should it not be capable of discovering in the evil that hunted it down the general evil of humanity? Should it always protect itself against entering with all forces into the battle of the warriors? Should it have the superhuman wisdom and self-restraint to distinguish in this general surge the path that is its own special path from the path that looks, almost to the point of confusion, like the striving of the warriors? That only so few, not all absolutely good, Jewish youth walk the paths of European-organized international Socialism—that is the biggest curiosity that affects Judaism today.

And in taking this course, and this selection, year by year Judaism loses a share of its best offspring. All those who are unable to wait, who consider the redemption of humanity a direct, undeterred possibility, among those for whom a kind of mechanical, inorganic conception of humanity steps toward the impatience of youth; all those who do not believe in paths and separate kinds of people and who believe that along with borders, people as distinct entities will fall; all those who wish to have an effect, at once and in an unmediated capacity, in the widest and largest sense, who do not want to see as the goal of their deed first the narrow, then the bit wider, and finally the all-encompassing, and who do not wish to carry out the deed for its sake alone, also not in and of itself alone, but rather in the most expansive substance; all whose brothers are the absolute human being; all who love either Russian tradition or German tradition; all who believe in the ancient mission of Judaism and of humanity, who believe, just as Paul is said to have won over the Jewish Christians and become, in succession of the prophets, the apostle for the people of the earth, that they too should be carriers and exercisers of the Jewish task for humanity, the task that says: clear the way so that there will be justice. Such people feel as though they are in possession of the Jewish mission and essence, and in debate they refer to the scriptures. And who could refute them?

And so at first they stand in all camps of the social revolution: in the democratic camp, which would like to achieve the goals of Socialism by way of the growing insight of humankind, of instruction and the force of proof, as through the firm belief in the inevitability of economic laws and changes without violence: justice on earth (and how very Jewish is this rejection of violence!); and in the dictatorial-Communist camp, which thinks it knows that only power, only commands, only force of strict ideology among human beings can help toward gaining control. That they, as Moses did before them to the wrangling people, are able to tame the hopelessly unruly ones; that through the feat of justice blood should also be spared, the same blood that was spilled into the sea during the reign of injustice; that they, servants of the prophets and of the idea of justice, for their pure service and from the nature of humankind, should be exempt from acts of tyranny and horror, in order, for the well-being of the other people, to pay them back for the sins they have committed against the Jewish people, the symbol of all the oppressed and on whom all the evil, destructive, unformed instincts of these other people became abundantly apparent during two thousand years of agony, blight, disgrace, and bloodshed—so that the disaster should be atoned for and, only in accordance with this helping and doctorly role into which it was forced by the other people themselves, so that true recovery should become possible. Revenge is an involuntarily produced venom for the healing, the

agony of the Jewish people, in order that it may become hard and merciless for this cure, which no other less scorched and pounded kind of
human being would be strong enough to perform; terror out of goodness, bloodshed out of wise compassion . . . there is much Old Testament
in this stance that appears horrific to us and eludes us, but it requires a
grand view of history and ethics for this type of stance to be able to con-
ceive of itself.

Yet how does the other branch of Jewish youth respond to its own
impulses? The branch in particular whose connection to Judaism and
the Jewish people is of such primacy and strength that it is neither able
nor willing to leave it behind? Those for whom Judaism and its responses
to the needs of youth are not too romantic, too "national," too petty?
Several possibilities open up here as well. This is the young boy for whom
Judaism is contained in his religious books. His eyes, small, inflamed
perhaps from countless awakenings in the night and weakened by this
for earthly matters, these eyes see behind the laws and the profoundly
sensible explanations of the Talmudists the infinite task: to study and to
live a life of learning. Poor, clumsy, he rejects with his defenseless mouth
the active life and the temptation of the times: he sees in the spiritual
life something more vital and eternal, and, filled with humility, he hopes,
in the battle with evil, to become an assistant and servant of one of the
great teachers. A touching purity stands above the lives of these young
boys, for the lesson according to them is first and foremost not that which
is gained for the sake of knowing, but for living. Indeed, their souls are
filled with the fear of not being able to follow the path that the great
sages once traveled, not from weakness, but because they demand something tremendous: to make their young lives, completely and utterly
without rest, identical with the commandments. There are commandments that one can only fulfill in the land of Israel, and hence, these
young boys shall go to Palestine. There is a commandment to marry
and to have children, and they shall do that. They shall explore the lessons of the Talmud day and night. And they shall wipe out all the "vices"

Bookish/
Jewry/Happy
poor
Ugly

and mortal urges, the true enemies of the human being—ambition, arrogance, violence, avarice, mendacity, hypocrisy—but not simply in
words toward others, but first within themselves, tirelessly and without
any form of pampering.

They, too, are heroes, these pupils of the yeshivas and Talmud-Torah
schools. They are Jewish "students," but one might search long and hard
for parallels among other people! One may find them, perhaps, in the
schools run by large Catholic monasteries. For these are the only monks
of Judaism and yet they are not even clerics, since the study of Talmud
and its literature affect one's entire life, and the rabbi is not a priest but
an adviser, a sage, and a judge. The yeshiva students are poor, but more
humble than poor; they are sometimes homely, but they are most certainly happy, happy even if they suffer from hunger, happy even if they
are troubled, if they suffer, cry out, or weep. Happy because they have a
path, and the gesture with which they turn away from the world is, without any form of nastiness or resentment, the sinking of their heads into
the open pages of their book. There is no sacrifice in this act, since they
much prefer the book, as it makes them happy. It goes without saying
that their intellect is of unimpeachable clarity and acuity. They have a
way of not quite dissecting problems of intellectual distinction, but looking at them in such a regard that in its application it comes close to the
most modern philosophy. (That is why one occasionally finds the books
and even a portrait of Henri Bergson in the homes of the *Ostjuden;* one
of the most talented students of [Edmund] Husserl was an *Ostjude*.) Their
lives are fulfilled in a realm beyond politics, art, and handcraftsmanship.
It is contemplation—a kind of wrestling, purifying, forward-moving Jewish contemplation. And the fiery wrath strikes down upon them only
when they collide with their opponent: with the profiteer, the man who
is nothing but a dealer.

This character does exist, and there are Germans who have discovered him in the East. There is nothing else to say about that other than
that the Westerner goes abroad with patterns in mind taught to him by
the newspaper that he reads and the school that he attended. He sees in

Serbia, the country of the most noble and endearing Western Slavs, parasites; in England, where ancient culture is still considered vital, where education still affects the entire human being, and where for the worker the most humane *standard of life* is made possible through radical social legislation, he sees sports and *business;* in Italy, dirt and harmless swindling; in Germany, fidelity and a sense of honesty; in Russia, alcoholism; and among the *Ostjuden,* groveling servility, laziness, haggling, and endless misappropriation of funds. That they, such observers, got involved only with Jews that were worthy of their kind, what do they know about that? That they found the Jew that they needed and expected, why should they suspect it? Oh, just as other kinds of people have their young lechers and murderers, we have our young hagglers and dealers for whom everything that has to do with rising up, with reputation and power, is for sale. We have those who, without any relationship to the possessions, without any feeling for the honorable nature of fidelity and conviction, without any shame, see in everything its cash and surplus value. They push and they cheat; today they peddle women, tomorrow leather goods, and the day after tomorrow political news. We have them and hate them. They are monsters and yet they are rarely like monsters, but rather frequently like somebody in monstrous times. A laborer who, lost in drink because he is denied the wage that he has long earned, kills his boss to keep from drinking himself to death, but first drives away his children so they do not see it—such a person is for us brotherly and closer to us than they are. But an officer who, protected by his uniform and entirely sanctioned by decree, has an old Lithuanian man and his eight sons shot before their house because in this same house he found an old shotgun that they did not hand over, who has them killed although they claim to have known neither of its presence nor of the order to turn it in—such a man who performs this deed as a cog in the machine of megalomania and who sees in it the fulfillment of his duty is more distant to us than the moon and more despicable than a white slave trader.

However, where the young Jew is not driven by a new idea about himself, where he does not find his form of observance in the immersion in ancient tradition—the average young Jew is not happy in his own skin, even if he does not feel restlessly enslaved by the frenzy of his trade and profession. This chin, bearded and covered, does not exactly stand fresh and young upon his neck; the restlessness of his eyes is well known to us, his depleted face reveals the total lack of relaxation, of the very ability to rest, and his mouth is so animated, so distraught, so very bare . . . Thoughts circulate ceaselessly in his mind, unceasingly the inner ear listens to himself, as if the heart of humankind were transposed into his brain and into his ability to hear. He absorbs by conceiving in words what is presented before him. (That is why the Jew moves so easily into the fields of journalism, literature, and legal advocacy: the word, the spoken word dominates.) He processes and he produces while speaking. The method of Talmud study, to pronounce all dependent and incidental words, derives from this compulsion; it creates orators and teachers. The constant alertness of this type of person sets him in hopeless opposition to the standard, to the masses. He cannot relate to them; for him, they are just the background of a conversation. But the great river and the sea, roaring and restless, are familiar to him: they feed into him. Chess is his most sublime form of relaxation, cards his most common, a densely populated, conversation-filled cafe is his locus, which even in the din of a rustling night seems fundamental. (How nicely all these cities are surrounded by nature, Kovno, Grodno, Vilna, even Bialystock—if only the summer custom of the Russian dacha, or country house, would not predominate—and if only the most lyrical children would move there?)

For this kind of Jew, his body is not present merely as representative of his health—by which it is often ridiculously pampered—nor as a measurement of self-worth. Here the sexual ethos takes revenge on the individual man, just as at the beginning of marriage, as seen earlier, it did on the woman. The vital worth of man experiences a crisis: strength, dexterity, the joy of strolling, physical exercise, elasticity, physical youth, healthy physical beauty. The clear, soulful, and noble beauty of the

mature man, and of the old, has as a youthful preliminary stage a cerebral beauty that sparkles from intellectuality. But the simple precious beauty that befits the youth so enthrallingly—often seen in girls, and with children all over—is missing among these young men (perhaps only during such an epoch devoid of young men as that of our current occupation) more frequently than among the Russians or Europeans. Taking pleasure in one's body, the happiness of nudity, bathing for its own sake: all this is not possible in the ghetto. And since erotic culture makes body culture mandatory, one might understand why, in accordance with the laws of nature, in every generation aesthetically sensitive Jewish girls resort to non-Jewish or Western Jewish young men. I believe that I hear outraged voices that damn the Jewish heathen who dares to speak of such ancient, such Greek values in the name of love, and I casually nod my head at those who grumble. There once were such currents in Judaism, which found their expression in the "Shir HaShirim" [Song of Songs] and others which culminated in post-Pauline Christianity. Which of these is more Jewish is not left for me to decide. I choose the first and see clearly that much of the youth here in the East and in Palestine proves me right. It will depend on transforming the "evil urge" par excellence into a good force, on regaining the naturalness of the senses, and on easing the nasty obstinacy that in the Nordic climate derives necessarily from the sexual views of late Judaism into what in Southern lands is more naive, more Mediterranean, more cheerful. To speak with Nietzsche, "Il faut reméditerraniser le Judaisme."

Does the Mediterranean nature of the Jews have something to do with their talent for the art of theater? It is certainly true that three or four different kinds of Mediterranean people have strong mimetic tendencies: Greeks, Italians, Spaniards, and the French. Jews have, or at least had, a mimetic talent whose distinguishing feature is not its ingenious depths, but rather the splendid general core of actors of average ability and their chief means of expression in gesture, language, and face. Thus, in terms of production and reception, the relationship between the Eastern Jews and the theater is extremely intense, and the ac-

tor himself is one of two very popular types of artist. One readily forgives him for having a beardless face; the folds and molds that he makes
with it, his exceedingly adaptable mouth, his animated and expressive
eyebrows, are looked at like a venerable uniform or a medal. The step
from being an amateur to being a professional actor, and that from being an actor to being a person without theater, is taken with a kind of
ease that is inconceivable in the West. The best Eastern Jewish acting
troupe—and theater still travels in the East—the so-called Camaraderie
of Vilna Actors, or the Vilna Troupe for short, consists for the most
part of amateurs who acted in forced military entertainment during the
war and whose achievement as an ensemble for performing naturalist
drama was so extraordinarily great that they remained true to their success afterward.

In spite of this success, little by little and for various reasons some of
the most talented "comrades" left the stage, simply disappeared. Now it
is indeed true that the value of a performance cannot be measured in terms
of its success, since the Eastern Jewish audience, which is easily excited
about anything Jewish, greets even bad acting troupes with sold-out
houses overflowing with applause. Yet the special role of the theater is
indicated by the participation of the otherwise critical Jew; it is still an
expression of national hope, for the rhythm of the people and their feelings are intensified and exhilarated by the performance of the actor. The
Jew feels represented, elevated, secured, and celebrated by the figures on
the stage, who appear in various guises of himself—even in performances
that we can only consider parody or comedy, or those that fall into the
category of operetta, the national singing folk play. What excites the Jew
so much is perhaps the original, magical interest of the people in theater:
that what occurs there upon the stage, ceremoniously displayed, are deeds
that represent the entire nation; that Jewish lives, so realistically depicted
(and yet as far as I am concerned, quite improbably put together) as when,
during the scene, they take a turn for the better and have the power to
turn the fate of the Jews in reality toward the good and away from the
destruction with which Jews constantly feel threatened . . . This is how

the scene strengthens its existential feeling and moves up with magical significance to rest next to the religious service and its representatives, next to the second folk artist, the chazan, the cantor.

The cantor needs to look neither young nor noble, his nose can be sensuously swollen, his face red and fleshy, aged not only by his beard, but puffed up with fat. He may come along self-contentedly, his eyelids heavy, like a pigeon underneath his sumptuous fur cap, but he has to be able to sing. His voice has to be metallic and, unconsciously and like a storm, it has to blast the ceiling toward the heavens. He is a fully productive and self-regulating singer when he stands before the holy ark, with the Torah in his arms, and like a fountain is pulled upward by his tones, tones that burst from his mouth, while the Torah is turned toward the congregation; or when, hunched over the pulpit, he gives his voice a timbre that is choked with remorse and hollowed out with wailing (he gives it artistically, a technical achievement that unfortunately is not prayer per se). At the same time, he is the carrier, the conscious carrier of the word, and it is his goal to bring the word to its full expressive potential. He is the contributor of an emotion that is no more an entirely artistic experience than it is entirely religious. He edifies the congregation and it in turn idolizes his voice, his ability, and his melodies. In this regard, he is the living symbol of the times. He crosses over between aesthetic and religious influence, radiant, folksy, naively vain, not entirely devoid of the joy in profit. He embodies the luxuriant expression of an intense natural talent which only seldom develops into a purely unmediated elevated achievement—and thus he is the expression of this generation, which, now roughly in its mid-thirties, represents the ending of an extremely decisive generation of Jews. Often for several years or decades he will go to the stage in order to enhance Rigoletto and other figures from opera with his golden voice, often he will return to the synagogue later with a voice that has been partly used up, without the same greatness it had during his ascent, about which fathers tell their children and which quickly turns legendary—not a whole person, not an "amoliger

Yid" [an old-time Jew], but also not a figure turned toward modern times—a hybrid, a symbol.

But it would be tremendously unjust to separate this aspect from the Eastern Jewish youth of today, and that we do not wish to do. We still consider today's youth under the general symbol of children, since generations merge into each other like the voices of a fugue, and they are not clearly separate from one another. A past evening comes to life again. Storms hover above the city like today, as I write this. Muted brightness shoots a blue light into the night, trees struck by lightning grow still for a moment and then collapse boisterously, as if their fall smashed through the crust of this fiery bubble into the magma. Those were the times when we experienced the high summer nights of conviviality. When rain beat against windows like now and, perhaps, a sweet aroma rose from the freshly cut lawn, all around the city like the breath of a singing star. Yet we did not feel it behind the closed windows of house arrest, closed so that the midnight light would not call the attention of the military patrols and the police—there was drinking, talking, laughing, dancing around the tables. And the songs! The songs! Their melody contained the scent and melancholy of great wisdom, the sweetness of great wisdom like that of a soft, aged wine. They were songs of community [Gemeinschaftslieder] with the refrain that welcomed the good new week, since it was the day on which the holy Sabbath ended, and we celebrated Havdalah until midnight; they were rapturous songs intoxicated with God and the search for God and in the verse's climax there was just you! You! The songs stammered and marched up to the point of becoming revolutionary chants whose masculine tone paid tribute to the bold sacrifice made in prisons, to the righteous Jewish death. For the sake of an idea, and not for power! For the human being, and not for the rulers! Solitary at the silent gallows, and not in the unconscious trot led by the barrage of a convoy of comrades and the prospect of rescue. Such a feeling, what songs: they burst open all wellsprings! Storms loom over the world! One came from thirteen months at Verdun, had seen Serbia on the execution block and Lille in a state of occupation and strangulation: and there you cry out! Throngs of souls, throngs of revolutionary faces hanging from the trees, struck by lightning, like fruits of triumph: in these songs, you stood here, Jewish people. You had the salvation. You were young, your faith alone was not enough to reach the regenerative future of the people in the ancient land—over there where Western thought had also reached. Rather, it reached the regenerative revolutionary future of Europe, Socialism on earth. And although today we both understand different things under that term, since hearing your songs, my understanding also reaches in that direction.

Let us return. Songs, songs. Young Jews out of whom the past, present, and future emerge in song like prophetic clouds from the young cracks in old stone formations: CONTINUATION. Formative strength stems from you. Not the voices alone, the bodies sang as well, and they sang around us. Now and again, while singing, you break out of your individual self and you plunge back into the collective being of the people which is one and the same, even if it should change. Then you become, in an apparent wave, a gift toward our continuation, insofar as you feel connected to all those before you, and without this you would be nothing. Your being consists in the act of going forward and through this your presence is fulfilled. You are a piece of born melody, music whose metaphysical force is contained in the will of the world toward the future.

With music in his veins, the Jew stands in mysterious relation to that dark, flowing, moving element that is likewise called continuation and that is a creative demon. Generations approach it, generations fade away like an increasingly soft, increasingly slow bar of a melody. But just as often as a voice in a multivocal fugue reaches an end and becomes silent, a fresh breath of air, bright, cheery, and boyishly sweet, sets in at a high pitch and opens up the entire piece toward a new movement—often with a return of the previous theme, often with hitherto unseen variation, always with a movingly young, unspoiled, mighty ascent and blissful lightness, like the red dawn emerging from the darkness of the night. These are the voices of children for whom the old man is substituted by both of the great mysterious forces, death and continuation. And it is startling when, time after time, a theme bursts out of the bright young voices, a primal theme with which the great Jewish fugue should start to play violently, uncontrollably, restlessly, like the promise with which the people emerged out of the morning clouds of history: it plays the fortissimo "Canaan."

V.

Immersed in his book, his lips pursed from participating in the act, he sits in the sun with his upturned collar and he reads—no doubt a poor chap, whose life, even when supplemented with a resonant imagination, pushes on bitterly. And this is the way they all sit at some point, the young, the very young, and leaping from the springboard presented by the book, they burst out of the mundane. But they do not keep on reading. "This is the way it should be!" they cry out to each other. Life on earth should become the way it is in books: free, colorful, windswept, exciting. And yet it should not lead us away from Judaism! To what degree are my language, my ideals, my means, my gait, disposition, appearance, and spirit different from those of Lithuanians, Poles, or Germans? Related but different? I do not want to become like them, but rather to have just as much as they do, yes, more than all of them combined, for without the spirit of my forefathers they all would not have become what they are. But I, I have become what I am without the spirit of their forefathers! And if I want to, I will learn their traditions, in addition to my own, without giving up what I am! For I am committed to much more than they are—such foresight and such a distorted presence oblige me to want a lot! This does not have to be the prevailing mood of youth that has been raised in poverty and in an unjust and cruel environment, exposed very early to every form of life. The Jewish ideal of righteous life is in his blood, and at the same time shows the defiant and internally grounded will to keep his essence pure. Does that mean to live and to learn Socialist lessons in a Jewish way? Should not the core of Judaism, the stiflingly shrewd will toward self-preservation for the sake of Jewish duty, take on new forms in new generations, like a fencer who can deflect every weapon with which the zeitgeist resolutely attacks him? Yes, yes, yes: the youngsters had to take the step that took them from the mechanically conceived Socialist idea to that which is organically conceived. Socialism, carried forth in the everyday life of the Jewish people, produced the most varied degrees of pure representation of itself. To live in small settlements, without a state, in a communal, antipolitical spirit, under the principles of collective ownership concerning land and soil and with the decisive means of production of the Socialist spirit, in the land of our work and of our fulfillment—they range from a kind of Jewish Socialism, which is pure Marxism, so to speak, and its province of agitation, which characterizes the Yiddish-speaking people, up to a kind of pure Socialism which resembled the character of the startlingly strong human being and assassinated leader Gustav Landauer, who always found various degrees of an incarnation of Socialism that is still purer. And one need only pose the question: where is this building possible as a pure form of building, without having the threat of destruction looming over it from the beginning? One poses it in order to make sure that it is not a prejudice to say that the colonizing Palestinian Socialism is really a purer representation of the idea than every kind that first needs to destroy violently in order be able to build. The round wheel that rolls on its own, the true beginning is the symbol of every creation. All harshness, masculinity, power to generate, which any Socialism prone to violence must prove as a power of destruction, will need to be purged from our Socialism and thus turn it into a kind of pure building. Zionism may well have begun as a bourgeois movement, and today the bourgeois element may have the loudest voice next to those who are loyal to tradition. But its energy, its guarantors are the young Zionist Socialist associations and their voices make the overall impact. For what today is built, worked for, and created in Palestine is done by people who are shaped by this character, *Ostjuden*, who have been transformed by both of these formative energies, work and land, and whom the best of Western Jewish youth joins from the other side. One thing has indeed always been part of Zionism: the idea of Jewish renewal was already there in Herzl, even if it was not until Buber that the full magnitude of the idea was conceived of and taught as a duty, and in this regard, as in so many others, he was the first great teacher of modern Jewry. Renewal: that is what separates us from the others. To the bourgeois Zionist, this renewal remains a physical, possibly a national concern; for us, it is a concern of the human being in its entirety and in its deepest essence, a religious concern. And to the Jew who is faithful to the Torah, it can only serve as a guidepost "back to the Torah," to the entire code of law, to life as it once was. And the best of them look at it in terms of its grandeur and purity, and already today they live this life with glorious heroism, while we hear in ourselves the impulse and the voice announcing that renewal must bring in a new spirit and new form of life, bring in truth, which springs from the rhythm of future-oriented generations for whom the reinstatement of our defunct customs would necessarily have to have a romantic and artificially disorienting and inauthentic character. The spirit of community *[Gemeinschaft]* with which we now wrestle, in order that it should redeem us, has to create its own forms of fulfillment freely out of our lives. The names of God have to reveal to us new paths of life. For he exists again today, the unfamiliar God. "I shall be who I shall be." Should we wish to be chosen, to be named servants of that which is eternally transforming itself in the people?

Work and land—the effective forces were already manifest in the *Ostjuden*, land as a kind of yearning, work in its hard, its despiritualized and yet still also semi-joyful form. Young boy out of whose narrow face the brownish nobility of your race sparkles. You, thin figure of suppleness in your forlorn awkward frock, it is not the purpose of your conduct that you should sweep the chimneys of this little town as a master's apprentice. Rather, in the toughening up of your body, in the strengthening of

your arms, in the indefatigable exertion of your will, there lies your purpose. You, who have learned the harshness of work, you should not practice it in the soot of the chimneys, but amidst the aura of the sea, in the hot breath of the sun-scorched earth and in the aroma of a fever; and this, this work on the land will be that which teaches you the purpose of work! "Work is the supportive and formative act of the human being on earth, and in its treasures lies the service of God's property" (Buber). And it will give you something that you, young boy, know only unconsciously: the pleasure of your body, the exultant and bouncing joy in the service of your muscles and in the speedy rush of the blood in your nourishing veins, which are themselves capable of expressing the freedom of the human being. Whoever has never had his shoulders pressed against an iron bar with iron weight pulling upon it, never dug a pickax into dirt that is frozen solid, who does not know what sort of powerful and splendid servants human will and the human body are, he does not know himself, nor does he know the human being. The wild laughter in the face of material resistance in its crassest form is the most masculine laughter under the sun, and even the fatigue after this kind of exertion is more fruitful than any other kind; it can make one happy, when the worker is a free willing servant at work in a state of affirmation. You, who learned to squeeze your shoulders like a cat, through the narrowest of chimneys: you will learn to laugh the way that Jews have not laughed for generations, the laughter of your free-moving body will flash before your eyes and teeth, young boy, young boy! It will give back to you the body you once had, when Joshua was a blacksmith and Jochanan a cobbler, but does it need to be another person? When one places an Oriental cap upon you, child, are you not then looked upon as if standing before the walls of Sichem? Your body will then no longer be without light, without air, no longer suffocate beneath heavy clothes in barracks that are overcrowded with people or in toxic streets. When you are a man, it will still readily show that which it shows you as a child and that which among us is so startlingly seldom revealed: physical power and physical beauty. And if you grow up as a child who takes joy in work and learning to work, you

will receive two great favors simultaneously: you will grasp the virtue of productive activity and you will feel the spirit of true exchange. For only the person who exists without any relation to the heart of his material things, who gets hold of money without enlisting any effort, without being affected by the essence of this thing—how it was arduously procured or how it became riddled with worries—only he can sell things professionally for the sake of profit. For the human being, the freedom to buy and sell and have a fair exchange is appropriate, but a nation of dealers should be considered an illness for him. And although among the *Ostjuden* the laborer always made up the main faction of the people, among the Western Jews it is a different situation, and the easy life of the trader, devoid of manual labor, attracts in high numbers from among all people, also among the Jews. It is indeed a perverse hierarchy in which the businessman is worth more than the creative person, and the custom that was once observed in old villages, where only one person opened a store, and that same person was then robbed of his workforce—the old man, the cripple, and the widow—appears almost more just. We must restore order to the old world that has been turned on its head by these capitalist times into which the Jew—first partly forced, then very willingly—integrated himself; we must put this world back on its feet again, even if in the process we should need to go to the other extreme for a while. After the "easy life," the extreme very quickly balances itself out, for all people should need to learn of the damage done toward the Jew, those who forced the Jew into performing the most despicable of business transactions, their own world order gradually became infectious, but will finally be reversed and totally destroyed.

You shall not become a black marketeer or a haggling Jew, my son! Your childlike innocence, which radiates above you like the near holy grace of a young animal, will, as you become a man, be developed into the kind of trusting and friendly comradeship that often makes this powerful human being such an attractive type of human being and attractive type of Jew, as is already apparent today, not just in the East. We do not know if there is such a thing as an innate trader people, and we do not believe it; but we do know that due to economic legislation aimed against the Jew, he has been made into the consummate city dweller. Owing to social pressure and the example set, acculturation and allure, all of which have shaped him over thousands of years, it appears as though it could not be any different. And if indeed Jewish youth were capable of casting this aside, if Jewish workers could present themselves, through their mere will, as being down to earth, it would prove to anybody who wishes to believe at least that the primal essence of the people does not match this allure. It is not that we demand more insight, but that we expect it. A people is a living organism in which there exists a variety of forms of resistance in order to suppress the impulse toward spreading itself out in space and time, an impulse that every life must face. And if the taproot of a plant, during its upward push toward the earth's surface, hits a shoe sole, and it does not follow this injunction to stop its growth, but rather splits like a fibrous root into so many different strands in order to circumvent the obstacle and to spring together again into the taproot while still underground—everything is contained in this image, namely, how we became traders and how we will stop.

Children are indeed more malleable than anyone else. They are even capable of learning how to resist. How much more willingly they follow directions that merely wish to lead their impulses into the realm of the pure, the cheerful, the active. Nothing is easier than healing them of their madness and their wish to own property. For the desire for property— which even an animal has in its relation to it own den, marking its own nesting place and place for food—has degenerated in the human being to such a degree that it has been made into the demon on earth. Where have the times gone since the soil and fields, forests and water, meadows and pastures, were common property, when the human being could not even approach these general things with the desire to cut them out and have them for himself, for the common goods of all these conditions were indeed spared from the mere impulse! We must limit once again the omnipotence of property to that which is a necessary possession, to living space and clothing, to basic equipment and tools for life. We must teach the human being once more that the soil belongs either to all or to God and the working machines belong to everybody for whom they are of use. The railways and rural roads, factories and the soil itself must, in a well-founded communal existence, belong to all. And this condition, unheard of today, would seem just as natural, after a generation, as common property in those transportation concerns appears to every child today. How much more carefree the human being would grow, how much better! For honestly, this boundless desire for property is a more destructive devil for the human being than every other extremely degenerate desire, perhaps with the exception of the violent desire for power—and since the human being is not good, but rather can become better, the reduction of the sphere of possible goods that he can own makes him better. As a people of the most extraordinary contradictions, however, we have in us not only the extreme "owner," the capitalist from the newspaper, who controls the opinions and needs of the people, but also his counterpart, the Communist worker in Palestine and Russia.

Isn't this boy sitting here, for now young, like the pointer on the scales in their midst? Does passivity not speak out from his helpless manner, which can be called upon in the service of any direction of the verdict? Yes, if one were only able to allow him not to stop; if not for time alone, and if life in today's cities did not have in its grip the horrible burdens of decay and of lifelessness, of the dull mechanization of every real humane relationship, and if they were made valid again forever. That is why we cannot remain silent, for the opponent never keeps quiet—he who has the power to lure us down his tortuous paths and who impressed upon us his distorted image of human coexistence! Although in the course of following our instincts and our knowledge we did not quite fall under his spell, what mediocrity came over us, what complacency with the conditions of our bourgeois environment! Who are we, anyway, today and here! We have to tell the children emphatically, do not become like us! Rather, become more, much more! Look at the restrictions we face and look at our incapacitation—not in order to judge us, but in order to do better. For it is not enough to have the best intentions and to love one's

neighbors—we have tried all this and we warn you to avoid doing the same—if at the same time one is capable of feeling fine during an era in which one does not even notice the terrible tension between intellectual culture and the extreme crisis of the proletarian existence. We, too, were optimistic, trusting, and altogether innocent children—and what became of us? We are partly to blame for the horror we face in our times. But at least our hands are free of blood and we never became "accomplices in the hatred," never exercised organized force on captured human beings. The land of the enemies was for us a source of reverie just like our own, and its possessions more venerable than ours. And yet, and yet! We did not do enough. We did not pit ourselves against it. We did not sense the evil, we bought into the lie, we did not fight against the evil . . . Nothing is accomplished by half-hearted or even active protection against defilement. Nothing is accomplished by purification of the soul alone. Children, you must fight against the evil, indeed fight against it and help us do good and suppress what is sinful. For if one day you were to sit here like us, crushed, weakened, dispersed, and kept from all that is good, once again redemption of the world would be postponed! God's carriages would be broken again and their wheels crushed, kept from their useful or graceful tracks.

Yet, you still have the strength and one may speak to you with confidence and one may look at you with tremors of emotion. Honestly, when dressed in your caps you look like the righteous warriors of the spirit, you are capable of glancing ahead, you are pioneers, sent by God into the plains and across the rivers! Boys, boys and you, too, girls: look ahead and do not turn back again after you have taken a good look at us! Your goal is the establishment of a just life. Your enemy is the demon of money, selfishness, trade, and the times in general. Your danger—one that very clearly tempts you and much more radically attracts you than it ever did us—is pride in yourselves. Your downfall is due to us, to us, who understand a great deal and were almost to become too clever to be able to hate. But hate, too, is a building block in the foundation of the temple; there is only one thing that is useless and that is self-admiration, which

threatens to render you altogether powerless and worthless. We expect from you that you serve the cause of humankind, just as you yourselves were served in the best of times, because you are Jews and this task has been assigned to you for as long as the Jewish people have existed. There is no other battle for God than that on earth, there is no other service of God than that in life with the people. Either all words of the law and the speeches of the prophets and of Joshua are meant literally, in this life and on this earth, or we all are worth less than plants or grain. Your eyes may wish to cast a sharp glance and never again see this as an entirely losing battle, but the human being must be helped and we are called upon, with everybody and before everybody, since we are older than you and have suffered so much. The path toward relief, however, is such that we first need to come closer to each other and, with clenched teeth, we need to create life anew for ourselves and for the entire body of people. For we need to recognize that if we want to offer relief to other groups of people—as we see them standing before their duties naively, blindly, and without guidance, helpless as far as knowing where to begin and with which grip of the hand—if we want to help them, because we love them so much, the young, noble, and dispersed groups of people, then we must recognize that we make them angry. We must recognize that we inflame the demon in their breast, the demon called "violence," like our demon "trade," and we show it the escape route on which it lurks despairingly. We do not lighten their souls, but rather darken them and enable them to circulate in blind rage, the soul of Edom! May every one of us see this and reflect upon it deeply in his heart. If, however, he then decides and says that the times are calling out for me, telling me that I should fulfill my deed here in this place, he may go there—one more victim.

Look at your defiant warrior glances, you Jewish boys! Your unfettered and vigorous hatred of violence and mutilation, which links you to the entire youth revival of Europe, is the rejuvenation elixir of the times. Indeed, there is much wreckage in the world, mountains of defamation, murder, robbery, and haggling, entire countries and people sold off, and people smother their own future, their possibility of flourishing, in blood,

robbery, decay. Every human being today, in his given post, is linked both to Hercules and Samson, and never before has a more warlike spirit aimed against the devil been needed than today. How fortunate that you have it in you! That you can pounce upon the devil like *rowdies* and heroes of a spiritual battle! Cowardliness and half-heartedness are widespread, and one's good will swells up everywhere as a reason for apology. Boys, that is not enough. Your strength has to join in. The manliness of man has to rise up, go there, and get to work. And because the apostles of war secretly stir up things all over, and spout their provocations openly, we cry out our credo directly to your face: we say aye-aye to war against drowning in blood! War against allowing our warlike spirit to degenerate into a servant of idiotic machines of destruction! Our manliness should once again, after having been desecrated in a hurricane of disorienting rage for five years, finally become a virtue. A handful of Jewish Socialists and Scandinavian polar explorers, American bridge engineers, English or German tropical colonialists, all have more manliness and pugnacious strength than an entire firing squad of Prussian army servicemen. There was more gallant bravery in Flaubert and Cézanne than in Joffre, Nivelle, and Foch. Like Karl Liebknecht, who stood against the hatred of an entire country, Rosa Luxemburg fought against the military spirit and its representatives, against generation after generation of officers, against the whole caste of human violators and executioners, and she was more manly, more combative, and of greater soldierly virtue than either Kluck or Ludendorff. For what a human being does when supported by a mass of people under his command, that doesn't count; what a human being does on his own, by himself alone, in solidarity with the spirit of life, that counts! Boys, remember the last days of Gustav Landauer, how he waited, alone and unshielded in a small cottage, for his fate to come to him and how he greeted it when it came time: "As it now comes to death, one must keep his head up high." Remember those brave souls and become brave in the face of laughter, cowardliness, and the rawness of a world that is roaring toward its end. Clench your teeth, straighten your neck, and think of the fact that you, too, are ambassadors of the spirit.

That maintaining order and well-being among people is your duty as well, and that the Jewish people is your orchard, an orchard that will be fruitful for you and will not disgrace you, so that the world will believe once again: "Salvation comes from the Jews." Oh people, you strange and glorious people, broken up like after a rain, bursting with sprouts like spring soil—whose heart does not open up with love when he sees you and become inflamed with anger about your essence in the Diaspora?

Who does not look at you, does not observe and absorb you, your eternal life, your spirit of all spirits, capable of every change, open to every form of purification! Who are you anyway, that after so many centuries your children are still playful and frolicking, pure, trusting and without pretense, talented, with cheerful wisdom and grace and modesty! You are children for whom the spiritual is relevant and yet who do not deny their childishness, children who are not devastated by the burden and misery of life and who, when faced with the corpse of their father, murdered by legionnaires, and the corpse of their mother, become silent and tough, but during their lives do not go mad or become consummate seekers of revenge, perpetrators of violence, or self-destroyers! In the faces of these children there is the answer to the question that has followed along, hidden behind all words up until this point: is the Jewish people embodied in the old man? And is the hardened or wise old man its symbol? No and no! If the eternally rejuvenated essence would be the nature of the old man; if the indefatigable beginning, the constant will to perform one's duty, the holy fidelity toward one's essence in the midst of renunciation were the nature of the old man; if fruitful ambivalence and constantly newborn doubt, if the will toward action and the eternally illuminated and eminently possible hope for a real, pure, human coexistence were the nature of the old man; if, as the goal of human beings on earth, the act of moving and being moved were ever the nature of the old man! Oh people, a youthful heart has formed in your breast, forever you stand before the times with a new, ardent hope. Oh people, you still believe in the human being, in the spirit, and in life! A child is your symbol, a young boy with a softly shaped nose, with a kind mouth and large, innocent eyes.

Isaac, who trustingly and gently stepped toward sacrifice and cried from the pile of wood; Jacob, who was preferred over his brother and who, fleeing into misery, ran into God; Joseph, who dreamed his dreams and who reported his brothers to his father and then went to them in a beautiful colored frock; Benjamin, who had to go to Egypt; and David, who had to take on Goliath. Young boys, always boys! Still to this day we cannot find other witnesses for you. Because you yourself are a young boy, Israel, an extremely young people, astray like the youth and striving for the right path, like youth once again, so that a voice calls out to you: "Come home, Israel, to your father, for you shall be consoled!"

Israel is a young boy on earth, innocent, disoriented, defiant, and ready to return home if somebody approaches him with the righteous and benevolent word to ease his shame. Listen, the times have begun to utter this word. It turns up in these times, inconceivable in and of itself—unaware of the strangeness of its beginning and ending—like a strange woman at the edge of the street who looks at you suspiciously as you sit there, young boy Israel, with your Russian soldier's cap placed crookedly upon your head, because for you she is foreign and faraway. She sees you and wishes to approach you, and she curses at you. But she then feels the unbelievable emotion rising in her heart, because she looks you in the eye, and the evil words begin to falter and, like an act by a holy magician, they reverse themselves into words of benevolence and solace and deep compassion: how beautiful your canopies are, Jacob, how beautiful your huts, Israel!

Oh, then your heart will open up, Israel, and you will shed tears of morning rain onto the soil.

Whoever should see your eyes shall have to console you. You bring out the good in each human being, and inspire it to be reflected. With your dark complexion and rounded face that is slightly gleaming, you approach the times, all times, fully and openly. And they catch a glimpse of all that is miserable in this people, shame and burned homes and the blood of the dead, but they do not reflect it, because instead they cry about it. For like Solomon's mirror, they are only prepared to reflect that which

is part of the essence, and that which is connected to those elements that are good.

Young Jewish boy, the sons of the earth should justify themselves before your eyes and, red with shame, they shall turn away.

Young Jewish boy, your eyes inspire us to take account of things, and when we do, there is almost nothing in our hands to serve as testimony for us. You, however, are our judge.

You are eternal, like Abel, who was conquered, and you hold court, a mild advocate for our deeds and the deeds of the human being. Gustav Landauer said to his murderers, you do not know how much you are incited toward violence. Time and again Abel speaks: you do not know what you are doing. And he forgives them.

Abel, young Jewish boy, eternal beginning, new spring: one morning, out of the wells of your eyes one shall create the elixir of life. In those Salomon-like mirrors of your eyes, the face of the Messiah shall be reflected, something that has certainly been promised to the people and to the earth, to bring peace and to reveal the goodness of humankind.

We shall not see him.

Then you shall be known as a friend of all mortal beings. Then, young boy, remember us fondly.

GLOSSARY
OF NAMES AND TERMS

Agnon, S. Y. (1887–1970): Famous Hebrew fiction writer born in a small town in Eastern Galicia. Arrived in Palestine during the second *aliyah*, or second wave of Jewish migration (primarily from Eastern Europe), in 1908.

Aleichem, Sholem (Sholem Rabinowitz, 1859–1916): Ukrainian-born Yiddish novelist and famed storyteller. Perhaps best known for his Tevye stories of the late 1890s, which would be adapted in the popular musical and film *Fiddler on the Roof.*

Amalek: Son of Eliphaz and his concubine Timna, grandson of Esau. He is said to be the ancestor of the Amalekites, the fierce tribe that attacked the Israelites from the rear on their way to the Promised Land at the time of the Exodus from Egypt. The Amalekites became known as the bitter enemies of the Israelites and came to represent the archetypal enemy of the Jewish people in each generation.

Asch, Sholem (1880–1957): Polish-born dramatist, critic, and novelist who published his work primarily in Yiddish and belonged to a group of strident defenders of Yiddish as the true Jewish national language.

Baal Shem Tov (Israel ben Eliezer, 1698–1760): Literally, "master of the good name." The founder of Hasidism, born in a small Ukrainian village on the Polish-Russian border.

Bergson, Henri (1859–1941): French philosopher, author of *Matter and Memory* (1896) and *Creative Evolution* (1907). He won the Nobel Prize for Literature in 1927.

Beth Am: Literally, "house of the people," a designation for locations/

functions that are included in the general term "synagogue." See Beth
Ha-Midrash.

Beth Ha-Midrash: House of study, discussion, and prayer. Zweig also refers
to it by the Yiddishized term *Bessmedresch.*

Bialik, H. N. (1873–1934): Russian-born Hebrew poet, writer, and critic considered one of the greatest poets of the modern period.

Buber, Martin (1878–1965): Viennese-born Jewish theologian and philosopher.
Founded and edited *Der Jude,* a cultural journal; author of *Ich und Du* (*I and
Thou,* 1923). Fled from the Nazis to Palestine in 1938.

Chagall, Marc (1887–1985): Russian-born modern painter known for his abstract portraits of East European Jewish life.

Fliess, Wilhelm (1858–1928): German ear, nose, and throat specialist who col-
laborated with Sigmund Freud on various psychoanalytic projects.

Gemara: Literally, "addition." The main body of the page in the Torah, occupying its center and printed in formal block letters.

George, Stefan (1868–1933): German modernist poet and critic known for the
faithful and influential circle of writers who gathered around him.

Gray, Dorian: Title character of Oscar Wilde's *The Picture of Dorian Gray* (1890),
a young fellow who, in keeping with the trend of European decadence,
rates beauty over morality.

Haman: Biblical figure from the Book of Esther, chief minister of King Aha-
suerus and heir to Amalek, whose anti-Jewish policies and ultimate downfall are recalled each year during the Jewish holiday of Purim.

Herzl, Theodor (1860–1904): Founder of modern Zionism, critic, journalist,
and author of *Der Judenstaat* (*The Jewish State: An Attempt at a Modern
Solution of the Jewish Question,* 1896).

Husserl, Edmund (1859–1938): German philosopher, educator, and leading figure in the field of phenomenology. Author of *Ideas for a Pure Phenomenology*
(1913).

Kluck, Alexander von (1846–1934): Commander of the German First Army,
responsible for an aggressive and successful offensive against Belgium and
for the near defeat of France in the First World War.

Kropotkin, Peter (1842–1921): Russian anarchist and Communist theoretician
whose publications include *Conquest of Bread* (1892).

Landauer, Gustav (1870–1919): Author, critic, anarchist activist, and theorist.
One of the founders of Die neue freie Volksbühne in Berlin in 1892; editor
of *Der Sozialist* in 1893–1899 and 1909–1915; founder of the Sozialistische
Bund in 1908; murdered by counterrevolutionary troops in the fall of 1919.

Liebknecht, Karl (1871–1919): Socialist party leader and founder, with Rosa Luxemburg and others, of the Socialist underground Spartakusbund (Spartacus League), later the German Communist Party. Executed by the German government without trial.

Ludendorff, Erich (1865–1937): German general in the First World War; chief of staff under Paul von Hindenburg. Masterminded numerous battle strategies. Later participated in Hitler's Munich Putsch of 1923.

Luxemburg, Rosa (1871–1919): Polish-born Socialist, author of *Sozialreform oder Revolution (Reform or Revolution,* 1900), and advocate of the mass strike. A co-founder of the Spartakusbund (Spartacus League) and, like Karl Liebknecht, executed by the German government without trial.

Mishnah: The entire body of Jewish religious law that was passed down and developed before 200 C.E., consisting of six orders.

Moykher Sforim, Mendele (1836–1917): Pen name of Shalom Abramovitch, the so-called father of modern Yiddish literature.

Peretz, Yitzhak Leyb (1852–1915): Hebrew and Yiddish writer born in a small town in southern Poland. Became a major figure in Jewish modernism and secular culture in Eastern Europe. Known—with Mendele and Sholem Aleichem—as one of the founding fathers of modern Yiddish letters.

Rashi (Solomon Bar Isaac, 1040–1105): French-born medieval commentator on the Bible and Talmud known to this day as one of the most insightful Jewish exegetes.

Schneur, Zalman (1887–1959): Modern Hebrew-Yiddish poet born in Belorussia who earned a strong reputation among secular East European Jews at the turn of the century.

Sichem: City of central Palestine referred to in Genesis.

Tolstoy, Leo (1828–1910): Acclaimed Russian novelist perhaps best known for *War and Peace* (1863–1869) and *Anna Karenina* (1877).

Waad: Jewish political diets established in Poland in the last quarter of the sixteenth century, composed of deputies who were elected by the kahal, the council, or by minor diets comprising a greater number of councils. A *Waad* took place every year and lawfully regulated the domestic life of the Jews, distributing state taxes and representing Jews in all state affairs.

WEIMAR AND NOW: GERMAN CULTURAL CRITICISM

Edward Dimendberg, Martin Jay, and Anton Kaes, General Editors

Text: 10/15 Janson
Display: Janson
Compositor: Integrated Composition Systems
Printer: Maple-Vail Manufacturing Group